AREA
SATURATION
PATROL
A POLICING STRATEGY THAT WORKS

GLENN D. FRANKOVIS

Copyright © 2014 by Glenn D. Frankovis

ISBN: 978-1495316135

Published by Lemon Press in conjuction with Badger Word Smith

www.badgerwordsmith.com

www.lemonpresspublishing.com

Frankovis, Glenn D.

Area Saturation Patrol / Glenn D. Frankovis – First Print Run

1. Police Procedural — United States — Non-Fiction

TABLE OF CONTENTS

FOREWORD

In an attempt to address quality of life issues and reduce urban blight and the crimes that go along with it, I was a founding member of the Milwaukee County District Attorney's Office's Community Prosecution Unit. This unit assigned prosecutors to neighborhoods to work in conjunction with citizens and the police to combat issues that were most concerning to the neighborhood. I was fortunate to be assigned to the Harambee & Williamsburg Heights neighborhoods which were located within Milwaukee Police District #5. One of the issues that plagued both neighborhoods was open air drug dealing. Fortunately for me, the Captain of District #5 was Glenn Frankovis. Under the direction of Captain Frankovis, we assembled a unit of officers, squads, & prosecutors to respond immediately to citizen complaints of drug dealing. These area saturation patrols completely changed the game in those neighborhoods. A number of citizens in the neighborhood were given a cellphone number and would call when they saw drug dealing actively taking place on neighborhood streets. Upon receiving the information, our unit would immediately converge on the scene, completely catching the bad guys off guard. Since residents were so afraid, these open air drug markets had operated basically unchecked, but they were no match for these area saturation patrols. It became so successful that residents were begging for these patrols in other neighborhoods.

The best part for me was that we took neighborhoods, where residents were not involved with the police, and turned them into neighborhoods where residents were active participants and immediately saw the impact of their association with the police. The saturation patrols made the residents feel safer, and no longer feel like prisoners in their own homes. During our time using the saturation patrols, we made 100's of arrests, secured many convictions, recovered numerous guns and drugs, and engaged a community like never before. To this day, I will run into citizens from those neighborhoods, and they still talk about the work we were able to do under the direction of Captain Glenn Frankovis.

Judge Derek C. Mosley
Former Milwaukee County Assistant District Attorney

TESTIMONIALS

The ASP operation was a useful tool during my time as a police officer for the Milwaukee Police Department. As a regular "street" cop, your daily ability to proactively fight crime and deter the criminal elements in your city, town or county can all be tied to calls or "hitches" you have to take throughout your shift.

The ASP concept freed up numerous squads and police officers from being tied to these calls for service. This in turn let the officers engage in active police activities, like FI stops (field interview stops) and more in-depth police investigations. The police officers were allowed the freedom during ASP operations to stop and talk to the citizens and find out what was happening in their neighborhoods and districts. This in turn fostered an atmosphere of cooperation between the law-abiding citizens and the police officers that patrolled their neighborhoods. The citizens trusted the officers with information because the ASP concept allowed the officers and citizens the time to build up this trust. The criminals were also kept off balanced because they never knew when the ASP patrols would be out in their neighborhoods.

The ASP concept should be one that all cities and towns, whether major metropolitan areas or small townships, should utilize to build up police and citizen relationships that are all too important when fighting crime in our country. The ASP concept is a proactive measure in our fight against crime.

Michelle A. Stelter,

Former Milwaukee Police Officer (1996- 2002)
Former Special Agent for the Federal Bureau of Investigations (FBI) (2002-2006)
Current Senior Surveillance Specialist for Department of Defense, Air Force Office of Special Investigations (2006 to present)

GLENN D. FRANKOVIS

Marquette University's Department of Public Safety became a vital partner in fighting neighborhood crime, alongside the Milwaukee Police District 3 officer because of the vision and clear team-oriented approach Captain Glenn Frankovis expected of his officers and Command Staff. This university continues that close partnership today because of what Captain Frankovis instilled years ago and has carried on today. Trust and confidence between our officers has never been higher, and the crime statistics show it! Incredible leadership like that of MPD (Ret) Captain Glenn Frankovis only comes by "once in a lifetime" in policing.

Chief (Ret.) Larry Rickard

Marquette University
Department of Public Safety
Now Lynn University
Department of Safety and Security

At the core of Operation Street Sweeper, was the willingness of law enforcement to communicate with community residents. Instead of writing off an entire neighborhood as "bad", Captain Frankovis, his command staff and officers on-the-street understood that only a small percentage of inhabitants held the community hostage. A liaison with an anti-crime outreach program called Community Partners which was a product of a DOJ WEED & SEED effort was forged. Door-to-door outreach workers were able to directly contact Street Sweeper command staff, providing up-to-the-minute neighborhood observations. The Milwaukee Police Department strategized with and listened to recommendations from the Community Partners outreach staff, prioritizing what needed to be done to increase the community's quality of life and sustain positive resident involvement. Providing an immediate response to resident concerns resulted in substantial grass roots support for Operation Street Sweeper, which included inconveniences such as blocked streets, random vehicle checks and increased surveillance. Every successful action that eliminated a "hot spot" or drug house or a "family" that trashed the street boosted the willingness of residents to collaborate with the police. Finally, someone was paying attention to their neighborhood, their personal and financial investment and their need to have a quiet, calm community.

Susan Kenealy

Program Manager
WEED & SEED-Milwaukee/Community Partners
1995-2005

INTRODUCTION

On July 3, 2011, a group of young blacks—estimated to number about 60--went on what was described in a Milwaukee Journal Sentinel article as a "weekend rampage," beating and robbing "a smaller group that had been watching fireworks from Kilbourn Reservoir Park." Prior to this confrontation, this group had looted a gas station nearby. The article reports that police were "also seeking more information on a series of beatings associated with six armed robberies or strong-arm robberies against 11 victims" in the same area.[i]

In December 2011, Matthew Quain was returning home from a trip to the grocery store when he was brutally attacked by "a group of loitering young people" in what was then being called the "Knockout King" or simply "Knockout." An Associated Press article by Jim Salter reported, "Scattered reports of the game have come from around the country including Massachusetts, New Jersey and Chicago. In St. Louis, the game has become almost contagious, with tragic consequences. An elderly immigrant from Vietnam died in an attack last spring." The article included a statement from St. Louis Police Chief Dan Isom who said, "The city has had about 10 Knockout King attacks over the past 15 months."[ii]

A December 29, 2011, Milwaukee Journal Sentinel article began by stating, "Spurred by a recent trend of violent incidents involving groups of youths, Milwaukee-area residents and law enforcements officials are turning to social media to nip disturbances in the bud. Residents, police and mall officials worked together earlier this week to prevent fighting and looting at Mayfair Mall in Wauwatosa (a suburb of Milwaukee)." The article went on to refer to the July 3rd Riverwest attacks of random people and an August 4, 2011, incident in which bands of roving young blacks attacked people at the Wisconsin State Fair.[iii]

Similar incidents have been reported in Chicago and elsewhere around the country with the most recent trend being reported throughout the media as "The Knockout Game," in which a victim is randomly selected by one or a group of thugs and attacked without warning. The idea of "the

Knockout Game" is to hit the victim so hard that he/she is knocked unconscious. Often the attack is videotaped for display on social media sites.

A December 6, 2013, *New York Daily News* interview of returning New York City Police Department Commissioner Bill Bratton included a quote from him in which he said, "We'll attack trends like knockout the way a doctor goes after a basal cell before it becomes a melanoma....That's what we did with the wolf packs of the late 1980s and early 1990s. Go after them aggressively."[iv]

Please keep these references in mind while reading about the Area Saturation Policing (ASP) Concept. Herein, I explain this strategy and how it was employed. In the Milwaukee Police Department districts I commanded, ASP became the law enforcement philosophy of no-nonsense policing that addressed violent crime without adversely affecting the response to calls of a more basic nature. Also keep in mind that whenever I use the word "thug" in this book, it is meant to describe that element which uses intimidation and force to take whatever liberties they want and to disrupt the quality of life for decent, law-abiding people. Every community has had to deal with someone who fits this description. Smaller communities may have only one bully who can be dealt with by their local law enforcement officers without much effort. However, when dealing with groups of thugs a different policing strategy needs to be employed or cities can end-up like Camden, New Jersey, where cops have been attacked by thugs as reported in a recent *Rolling Stone* article, *Apocalypse, New Jersey: A Dispatch From America's Most Desperate Town.*[v]

In his article, Matt Taibbi writes about a change that took place to improve police services and quotes a "local junkie" who told him "These new guys, not only will they get out of the car, they'll haul you in just for practice."[vi] Taibbi also makes note of the new technologies, such as the Shotspotter, which "hears" and then triangulates shots being fired and dispatches resources to the specific location from where the gunfire emanated. Yet an overall strategy of preemptive policing is something that has not really been discussed since George Kelling's and James Q. Wilson's landmark study, The Broken Windows Theory of Policing.

The chapters of this book explain and examine a very successful policing strategy and enforcement philosophy that I implemented in two police districts I commanded as a captain with the Milwaukee Police Department. This plan incorporates elements of "Broken Windows," as well as a strategy I called "Preemptive Policing." Moreover, I will explain how my philosophy of policing evolved into an extremely effective means of making neighborhoods safe. Implementing this policy is dependent upon building trust and confidence with the residents of troubled neighborhoods through regular meetings and the delivery of timely services.

During my time with the Milwaukee Police Department, I observed and listened carefully to those leaders willing to share their knowledge and sifted through what worked and what didn't work in order to build on the foundation laid by others. The knowledge I gained was also built from innovative concepts and strategies employed throughout the country including various articles on policing strategy such as The Broken Windows Theory of Policing by George Kelling and James Q. Wilson.

A study of military history and successful leaders of the U.S. armed forces—like Generals George Patton, Douglas MacArthur, and Norman Schwarzkopf as well as successful college and professional athletic coaches—rounded out my research on the subject of tactics and further influenced the concept of the Area Saturation Patrol theory of crime suppression.

Having learned from the successes and failures of the past, and at the urging of several of my friends, including Steve Spingola, a retired MPD Lieutenant of Detectives and the current chair of the Criminal Justice Studies program at Gateway Technical College, I decided to share what I consider to be an extremely effective concept of fighting crime in cities. It is my hope that the information contained within these pages might serve as a blueprint for others to consider when pondering crime fighting strategies tailored to their particular communities.

Regarding the sharing of knowledge, legendary college basketball coach Bob Knight made note of the notion in his book, *Knight-My Story*. "What he [a former coach] represented to me in this case was the responsibility a teacher has to share with others whatever he has come up with that he found to be of some benefit," Knight wrote. "When later I was in a position to do that, I always did. If we were doing something that people were interested in, I never held anything back at clinics or in conversations with fellow coaches, especially young ones."[vii]

Within these pages, I will discuss my idea of what leadership is and include examples and quotes from influential figures of the past. I will further explain the policing strategy and philosophy I employed during my supervisory career with the Milwaukee Police Department, which spanned a period of time from April 1981 to February 2004, when I retired. Over the course of my career, I modified this strategy to adapt to changes in the environment and to improve efficiency and effectiveness.

Anytime innovative thinking is introduced to a status quo operation, obstacles will be encountered and a leader will need to find ways to circumvent bureaucratic and/or turf oriented roadblocks. I will spotlight some of the hindrances that I encountered and offer suggestions how to deal with them. In the end, though, successful implementation of the kind of policing strategy and philosophy I employed hinges upon those within higher levels of the chain-of-command. An aggressive response to combat violent criminal activity requires buy-in from the chief-of-police and politicians who may, at times, have to run interference when the usual suspects, including the mainstream media, accentuate the gripes and complaints of the criminal element that the police are being too tough. If your chief-of-police is one that has years of actual street experience and/or appreciation for what it takes to fight crime, then this strategy will work as it is predicated on support from the top and throughout the command structure.

CHAPTER ONE

LAYING THE FOUNDATION

When I became a Milwaukee police officer in 1975, I was assigned to District Five, the border of which stretched from Lake Michigan to N. 20th Street; from North Avenue to roughly the northern city limits. At the time, District Five was considered one of the busiest police districts. One of the many things I soon learned was that district commanders throughout Milwaukee had what were referred to as "special squads." These special squads were comprised of plainclothes officers, who were handpicked by their sergeants to conduct follow-up criminal investigations based on the written reports of other officers assigned to patrol units.

These special squads served at the pleasure of the district commander and were not subject to calls for service from dispatchers. Consequently, special units could focus their undivided attention to resolving problems. These officers also worked closely with detectives assigned to District Five whose responsibilities encompassed the district's geographical boundaries. Because these "special" officers were not subject to calls for service, the district commander could direct their deployment and mission absent from outside interference.

District Five's early shift (4PM to Midnight) also had two units designated as "cover cars." These officers were responsible for handling assignments when patrol units, assigned to designated geographical sectors within the district, were out of service. When cover car officers were not on assignment they functioned much like a free safety in football; whereby they patrolled a much larger area than a patrol unit assigned to a specific beat and also provided backup to other officers when need dictated. I was assigned to a "cover car" during my tenure at the early shift at District Five and learned firsthand how effective it was to have the ability to roam from one squad area to another.

In October of 1978, I was assigned to the MPD's Tactical Enforcement Unit (TEU). Each tactical enforcement squad consisted of three or, in some cases, four officers.   TEU units patrolled throughout Milwaukee, and each would have responsibility for two to three Police Districts. The primary function of TEU was providing back-up for district patrol units responding to all major crimes.   When circumstances dictated, TEU officers would establish command posts (CPs) and perimeters, if and when a major crime turned into a tactical situation (armed suspects on scene; hostage situation, etc.).

On occasion, TEU officers were instructed to assist district personnel when addressing specific problems within a police district. On one such occasion, a Hispanic gang had established "turf" near a south side park where children played. Some of these gang members charged a "fee" for children of the neighborhood to use this public park. Due to calls for service and limited personnel resources, district officers were unable to provide consistent coverage of the park. It was TEU's job to provide that consistent coverage and take measures to resolve the matter.

The method of operation was to stop any "likely" suspects and, in general, discourage the activities of the gang members. This worked, however because we did not know the good guys from the bad guys our stops also included some good people which created hard feelings on the part of some people. It was one of those experiences that helped shape my later philosophy of establishing lines of communication through Neighborhood meetings when deploying special operations.

In April 1981, I was promoted to the rank of sergeant-of-police. I then spent the next six years as a street supervisor on the late shifts (midnight – 8 a.m.) at Districts Two and Six—the city's two south side precincts. Later, I was assigned to the MPD's Internal Affairs Division for two years where, among many other things, I learned just how out of touch one can get from crime fighting being away from street patrol. Afterwards, I returned to the TEU as a street supervisor in spring of 1989.

Less than a year later, fellow TEU Sgt. Fred Shippee and I were ordered by our commanding officer, Captain Jeff Bialk, to prepare a "summer initiative" operational patrol plan to address violent crime. Sgt. Shippee and I drafted a proposal to deploy our day shift TEU personnel in teams of three man squads to patrol selected hotspots during the late afternoon/evening hours, while the unit's night shift officers would continue their normal duties.

During this operation, I observed groups of juveniles and young adults who would either be standing on street corners or roaming the neighborhood. These "groups" seemed to have no fear of the police as we drove past. It became apparent to me that Sgt. Shippee and I had to alter our plan if we were going to effectively address matters of crime and disorder. On occasion, I directed all units to converge on a specific location in order to maintain superiority of numbers. Over the next several years, as my research in the area of tactics progressed, I made patrolling as a group standard operating procedure. This change greatly enhanced the safety of officers, citizens, and potential suspects, by reducing the likelihood of physical confrontations and the use of force.

In very early 1992, I requested a transfer out of TEU and was assigned to District #2 on Milwaukee's southeast side (covering roughly from the Menomonee River Valley to the City limits south and Lake Michigan to South 16th Street) where I served as a Day Shift Patrol Sergeant. Soon after my arrival, the District Captain (David Bartholomew) brought to my attention complaints he was receiving about a problem with gang members near a local high school and directed me to coordinate with a night shift Sergeant (Sgt. James Cleveland) to initiate a Directed Patrol Mission (DPM) to address the problem.

District #2 did not have a wealth of Officers and could not get consistent help from our centrally located Gang Squad, so we established two 3 man squads and staggered their hours so that they overlapped with one squad working 11AM to 7PM and the other working 3PM to 11PM. Their instructions were to seek out those who were terrorizing the decent residents and to summarily arrest them for any violations of City Ordinances and/or State Statutes. (A copy of our Department Standard Operating Procedure relating to the Summary Arrest is included in the appendix of this book.)

This was going to be a strict enforcement, no nonsense operation. Anticipating neighborhood concerns about the noticeable increase in police presence and an uptick in enforcement, I directed our community liaison officer, Kevin Obremski, to arrange a neighborhood meeting at the local library where I explained the operation and established lines of communication with area residents. At this meeting, I provided attendees with my direct telephone number and urged them to call, once the operation began, if they had any concerns. The only concern raised was by a skeptical woman who said, "We've heard all this before." I told her and the others present that, if they did not witness acceptable results within a few days, they should speak with me directly. Having provided the residents with all details except the number of Officers and their hours of operation, we commenced the DPM.

During the first week of the DPM, the officers assigned to the detail were handling a disturbance in the targeted area; whereby, I exited my squad car to monitor their progress. They made several arrests and, as I walked back to my squad car, residents who were standing on the sidewalk approached and thanked me for finally doing something about the problem people in their neighborhood. It was the first feedback that I had received from those in the area and it was very encouraging.

I then drove around the corner and saw a group of juveniles, who appeared to be in their early teens, congregating on a porch. As I drove past the group, someone shouted, "Fuck the police!" I turned around, parked in front of the house where they were congregating, and summoned the DPM officers. I asked the six officers to conduct field interviews and introduce themselves to the group. While the officers and the juveniles were getting acquainted, one of them began mouthing-off to me in an apparent attempt to impress his friends. He walked back-and-forth, profanely stating that the police could not do anything to him because he was "only 12". I then took control of his arm; walked him over to one of the officers; instructed the officer to take the youth into custody for state disorderly conduct; and to refer him to the Milwaukee County Children's Court Center. When the officers handcuffed the boy, he cried like a baby. The arrest must have made quite an impression. About a week later, as I drove past this same house, the same group of juveniles were sitting on the porch. This time they kept their mouths shut. The message was clear that the police were not going to tolerate disorder in the neighborhood, and the consequence for violating that message would be quick and firm.

When officers are busy going from one call for service to another, it is virtually impossible to address issues of disorder, which might ultimately lead to confrontations between groups and/or the intimidation of law-abiding residents. This type of disorder, if not addressed in a timely manner, empowers the block bullies and gang members, and gives residents the impression that law enforcement tolerates this type of unchecked behavior.

Over the course of the first month, District Two's DPM was an immediate success. The operation resulted in many letters of appreciation from the residents who finally—for the first time in years—felt secure in their houses and safe in their neighborhoods. (I have included copies of some of these letters in the appendix of this book). It is important to note that the residents expressing their sincere appreciation further related that regular calls for police service were not adversely affected by this DPM.

Knowing that this DPM and its activity levels would be challenged by some inside the Department, I assigned two of the DPM Officers to maintain accurate records of all activity generated by the DPM right down to the number of parking tickets and Field Interviews written. Copies of all activity generated, to include Arrest Reports, were to be made daily and kept in weekly folders contained in one monthly folder. Those activity folders were kept in the Shift Commander's Office should anyone wish to inspect them.

Sometime later I received a visit from a Gang Squad Sergeant who wanted to discuss the DPM with me. I knew this Sergeant and was more than willing to discuss the DPM and answer any questions he might have. I got the feeling that he really didn't want to be at District #2 talking with me about this subject but was just doing it because he was told to do it.

You see, this visit may have been more about personalities than about the normal internal jealousy. Being someone who didn't always follow the script, there were one or two people downtown in the Police Administration Building who were less than thrilled with me. I wasn't about to let that interfere with what I knew was working.

Unfortunately, bureaucratic turf related battles and internal mistrustfulness are not unusual in any organization, especially when leaders at one location initiate a successful operation absent the blessings of a few ego-driven personalities within the organization's power structure. Bob Knight wrote about this in his book Knight-My Story: "As long as I was in Bloomington I had a plaque on my office wall with a quote from General George S. Patton: 'You have to be single-minded, drive only for one thing on which you have decided….And if it looks as though you might be getting there, all kinds of people, including some you thought were your loyal friends, will suddenly show up doing their hypocritical God damndest to trip you, blacken you, and break your spirit.'"viii

I suspected that the sergeant from the Gang Crimes Unit was sent by his supervisor to explain that the "Gang Squad" was responsible for keeping tabs on gang members and that District Two was not sharing information. Since the DPM was ordered by my commanding officer, the matter at hand seemed more appropriate for a discussion between our individual captains. Regardless, I escorted this sergeant into the shift commander's office, showed him the activity folders, and explained their contents. I further related that he could look through the folders and take them to the Gang Crimes Unit, where he could make copies of anything he wished. My only request was that these folders be returned. I then asked the sergeant if the Gang Crimes Unit would reciprocate and allow me to view the information that their unit had compiled. "No," was the sergeant's response, which didn't come as a surprise to me. He left District Two and never did accept my offer to view our activity folders.

This is just one example of the pettiness and politics that I had seen within the MPD during the course of my career. In some cases it was just dogs being territorial, and, in other instances, it was payback for some perceived deviation from the company line. One has to wonder why such pettiness would be exhibited by any supervisor within a law enforcement agency which supposedly values the team concept of fighting crime.

On a side note, this DPM had been the longest such operation of my experience with the Milwaukee Police Department, and literally pushed gang activity into District Six, the area to the west of District Two. Success be damned, the DPM ceased on the orders of then Milwaukee Police Chief Philip Arreola after an incident involving an officer from District Six, who was being assisted by DPM officers. The incident involved an excessive use of force complaint against the District Six officer. However, because of the aforementioned internal triviality and a local Spanish newspaper's interference for some of the thugs on the DPM officers' radar screen, Arreola pulled the plug on this successful operation.

One of the district's early power shift officers, who was not the least bit intimidated by gang members, stopped several of them on the street some time later and asked them why they were back in District #2 setting-up shop. The officer reported that the gang members' response was, 'You're not fucking with us anymore.'

This is an example of the work done by the Officers assigned to the District Two DPM:

DPM 93-02: AFTER ACTION REPORT STATS

The following is a compilation of activity generated by (6) Officers assigned to DPM 93-02 from January 1, 1993, through December 31, 1993:

Field Interviews:	6,114
Traffic Citations:	1,968
Muni Arrests (Including Warrants):	2,171
Misdemeanor Arrests (Including Warrants):	2,067
Traffic Warrant Arrests:	483
Felony Arrests (Weapon related):	66
Felony Arrests (Non-Weapon related):	181
Narcotics Arrests (Including Warrants):	228
Curfew Violations (Includes Parent Responsibility):	56
Weapons Recovered:	158
Seat Belt Violations:	346
Pedestrian Violations:	159

Confiscated and/or Evidence:

Cash:	$21,668.95
Marijuana:	1,758.84 grams
Cocaine:	1,291.31 grams
Heroin:	20.00 grams

The numbers document our strategy to "nickel-and-dime" the people responsible for compromising the quality-of-life within the troubled neighborhoods of District Two. These results further illustrate what can occur when law enforcement establishes an inhospitable environment for the criminal element. However, the real measure of success came in the form of feedback from the law-abiding residents in these previously crime infested neighborhoods.

A similar operation was initiated in Indianapolis, Indiana and Kansas City, Missouri in the early 1990s with great success. It was reported in the Milwaukee Journal (from a New York Times, Associated Press article) on November 27, 1994. The article stated that police in those two cities were directing their efforts into high crime neighborhoods with the specific intent to "get illegal guns off the streets" and to reduce violent crime. "Night after night, teams of police officers here (Indianapolis) are being freed from answering routine calls and directed to patrol three high-crime neighborhoods, watching for any infraction that will give them the basis to search for illegal guns." Police Chief Steven Bishop, Chief of the Kansas City Missouri Police Department at the time, was quoted saying, "I don't know why it didn't occur to us to really focus on guns. We usually focus on getting the bad guys after a crime. Maybe going after guns was too simplistic for us." The article went on to say that "Traffic stops were the most productive method of finding guns with an average of one gun found in every 28 traffic stops...." The article also states that "The Kansas City project reduced gun-related crimes almost 50% in the area in which it was instituted...." [ix]

CHAPTER TWO

EARLY STAGES OF AREA SATURATION PATROL

In September 1997, I was promoted to Lieutenant of Police by Chief Arthur Jones and subsequently assigned to the early shift (4PM to Midnight) at District Five. Captain Tony Bacich—the former district commander, who had retired about a year earlier—had established a special unit similar to, but larger than, the DPM that I initiated at District Two. Captain Bacich called this group of officers the "Neighborhood Foot Patrol" (NFP) unit, in compliance with departmental directives in place at the time.

Captain Bacich was the commander of District Five during the reign of Police Chief Philip Arreola, who came to the MPD from the Port Huron (Michigan) Police Department. Arreola brought with him the flavor-of-the-day policing strategy, "Community Oriented Policing" (COP). The new chief's brainchild called for each district to establish teams of foot patrol officers to be as one with "the community." In reality, NFPs, as Arreola envisioned them, were little more than a baseball card/teddy bear/lock-your-windows feel-good program, which contributed virtually nothing to the suppression of criminal activity.

Captain Bacich, being one of the great outside the box thinkers on the Department, disguised his "Neighborhood Foot Patrol" teams by putting them in Squad cars to actually do real police work. It was a gutsy and brilliant idea given that he was not considered a favorite son of the power structure.

I only needed to make some minor changes in order to insert the style I had developed with the DPM while at District #2 and quickly made those adjustments incorporating my summary arrest philosophy for the entire Shift of Officers. Having come from 6 years of Day Shift operations in a relatively low crime south side District to a fast moving District #5 with Night Shift Officers, I had to readjust my thinking and adapt to this much faster pace. To facilitate that process, I began to include one night of patrol into my weekly duties to reacquaint myself with the District.

One evening, due to other demands, my captain, Dennis Drazkowski, instructed me to attend a meeting on his behalf with concerned neighbors who sought to discuss problems in their neighborhood. I listened to their concerns, paying particular attention to a familiar ring. A group of juveniles was charging neighborhood kids a "fee" to walk down the sidewalk through their "turf." The children being shaken-down were intimidated. Residents in the area wanted the police to promptly resolve the issues. I assured them that I would personally look into this matter. I then conveyed this complaint to Captain Drazkowski. I explained that officers assigned to my shift would address the problem in short order.

I visited the problem area to see, first hand, what was occurring and did find a group of juveniles standing on the corner in question. It was immediately apparent that this wasn't a neighborhood ambassador program set up to help old ladies cross the street. I called in the officers from District Five's NFP unit to conduct field interviews. The attention the group received from the NFP unit eradicated the problem. This type of overwhelming attention would not have been possible using district personnel subject to calls for police service.

Chapter Three

The ASP Strategy Spreads to Yet Another District

In March of 2000, Chief Arthur Jones transferred me to District Four, an area encompassing the far northwest side of Milwaukee, where I commanded the early shift (4PM to Midnight), Early Power (Noon to 8PM), Late Power (8PM to 4AM) and Late (Midnight to 8AM) shifts. There was no Area Saturation Patrol unit in place at this work location, even though problem areas existed throughout the district. After discussing the matter and receiving the approval of the district's commander, Captain Vince Flores, I implemented an ASP unit and incorporated the summary arrest policy. District Four was understaffed at the time, so I asked Captain Flores for permission to internally transfer officers from one shift to another in order to properly staff an ASP unit. The captain granted my request and provided a wide-latitude of discretion to develop the unit.

I soon discovered that some officers assigned to the night shift were unaware that the Milwaukee Police Department permitted summary arrests for municipal ordinance violations. They apparently had been misinformed on that subject while in the police academy. I had occasion to later discuss the subject with a ranking official—an instructor at the police academy, who went on to explain that summary arrests could NOT be made for municipal ordinance violations. I told him that I had been making summary arrests for ordinance violations since Milwaukee adopted ordinances in the mid-1970s. Moreover, MPD's Standard Operating Procedures (SOP) manual contained provisions for such arrests[x] (See copies of the Department S.O.P. in the appendix). Needless to say, we continued making summary arrests, but that wouldn't be the last time I needed to explain the policy to a ranking MPD official.

Although District Four was far from the high-crime and high demand for services District Five, the ASP unit was better equipped to tend to the problems of drug dealing and other complaints that needed the kind of constant attention that only a district special unit could provide.

CHAPTER FOUR

OPERATION STREET SWEEPER IS BORN

In February 2001, Chief Jones promoted me to Captain and gave me Command of District #5. The policing strategy and enforcement philosophy I had previously set in place on the night Shift had been allowed to diminish under the Night Shift leadership put in place in my absence, so I made a few changes and reestablished my policing strategy and philosophy.

Having Command of the entire District operation, I was now responsible for attending all weekly Department Staff and Crime Analysis meetings. This meant that I had to have complete knowledge of all that happened in the District as well as crime trends and plans of action. (This was known as Compstat, made famous by NYPD Chief Bill Bratton and written about in Jack Maple's book: Crime Fighter.)[xi]

As I had previously learned from those few times I had to fill in for my Captain when I was still a Lieutenant, Crime Analysis was as much about "Gotcha" as it was about identifying crime trends and implementing strategies to address these trends. I took that as a challenge and immersed myself in the job.

That "immersion" included such things as requiring copies of every arrest report generated by District Five officers, which then enabled me to familiarize myself with the who, what, when, where, why and how of each arrest. I also attended every neighborhood meeting I could and conducted an intensive and daily analysis of crimes committed within District Five. I further continued my concept of "management by wandering around," which began when I was promoted to lieutenant – a position which was considered primarily an inside desk job.

General George Patton was a proponent of this style of leadership.

"Commanders must remember that the issuance of an order, or the devising of a plan, is only about five percent of the responsibility of command," Patton wrote in his book, *War as I Knew It*. "The other ninety-five percent is to insure, by personal observation, or through the interposing of staff officers, that the order is carried out."

Patton was also an advocate of delegating tasks to qualified people, noting, "Never tell people how to do things. Tell them what to do and they will surprise you with their ingenuity."[xii]

"Management by Wandering Around (MWA)" for me meant that I saddled-up, usually on a Friday evening, and spent anywhere from 8 to 10 hours patrolling the streets in order to get a firsthand look at what the cop on the beat, as well as what the people at the district's neighborhood meetings, were experiencing.

MWA made me believe, very strongly, that high-ranking police supervisors who surround themselves with four walls and a door can lose touch with what their officers and the law-abiding members of the community are forced to deal with. Moreover, I noticed that many high-ranking police officials, even those who were outstanding street officers themselves, seemed to lose touch with reality once they became part of the MPD's command staff.

The dynamic many command staff personnel experienced during their time as street officers and what the brass observed "back in the day" may no longer be relevant to contemporary policing. To be sure, the basic tenet of policing remains the same, and that is to maintain law and order. However, a well-adjusted police commander understands that things change and subsequently adjusts his or her schedule accordingly to remain in touch with the changes. Of course, this involved much more than just observing officers in the field. Listening to the radio traffic and the interaction between the officers and the dispatchers is important. Problems in policing are not only external, and getting a firm grip on the internal issues makes them easier to address. Furthermore, when a district commander is working the street, officers and their supervisors take notice and adjust accordingly.

It is, however, important not to get in the way of what officers are doing. Street cops generally detest having someone looking over their shoulders and critiquing their every move. As such, I made it a point not to dismount and/or interfere with their investigations unless some direction needed to be given, which was rare for the officers used to the fast pace of policing at District Five. From the feedback I received, the officers liked my management style. Not only was I holding the officers accountable, but my presence also kept their immediate supervisors — the street sergeants — honest, as it is their job to manage the officers on patrol, not the district commander's.

MWA — Management by Wandering Around — had the added bonus of establishing credibility with the troops and with the good people from the neighborhoods, who I met with regularly. When residents would see the district's commander on the street, or when they heard me speak based on the personal knowledge of things that they've related, the residents — those who cared about the community — knew that they had buy-in from the captain, who cared about their problems. I found this a valuable way to build trust and confidence, which fosters cooperation in the effort to liberate troubled neighborhoods (notice that I didn't use the word "occupy", as that connotes that it really isn't their neighborhood but rather an area the police seek to control).

Sgt. Bill Potterton supervised District Five's Area Saturation Patrol operation and did a remarkable job, both leading the officers on regular patrol as well as our new "Street Sweeper" operation, which was an immediate success and recognized by Chief Jones. The U.S. Attorney's Office for the Eastern District of Wisconsin later submitted "Street Sweeper" for consideration by the U.S. Department of Justice Weed and Seed program's national recognition award (See the write up in the appendix).[xiii]

While I do not possess the MPD statistics to compare District Five calendar year 2001 to calendar year 2000 crimes, the enclosed charts[xiv] spotlight District Five's 2001 statistics. Our success was measured more by the satisfaction of the various neighborhood groups, which was brought to my attention by their leadership, correspondence, and telephone calls. Chief Jones, in a call he made to me in November 2001, indicated that he was going to transfer me to District Three because, as he put it, "I need you to do in District Three what you have done in District Five."

Chapter Five

ASP and Street Sweeper Introduced to District Three

In November 2001, I was given Command of District Three with a mandate from Chief Jones to reduce crime. At the time, the boundaries for District Three were N. 16th Street to the city limits west; the Menomonee River Valley to the south; and W. Center Street to the north. It was arguably the second busiest police district in Milwaukee, which meant that this assignment posed significant challenges. Having paid attention to the crime patterns in other police districts during the weekly Crime Analysis meetings, I was somewhat aware of the issues that required attention at District Three. What I also discovered when I arrived was a somewhat disorganized operation that focused more on management's concern for reducing overtime than officer safety and/or suppressing criminal activity.

During the first few weeks as the commanding officer at District Three, I learned that an active directed patrol mission (DPM) to address a localized crime problem was actually authored by a commander in the centralized Criminal Investigation Bureau (CIB), the fourth-floor location downtown where the majority of the MPD's detectives reported for duty each day. The manner in which the DPM was structured was problematic, as many of the officers assigned to it from various divisions and bureaus worked at centralized locations outside the control of the district commander. Moreover, the members of these non-District Three units typically were not present at noon roll calls, which I discovered shortly after l arrived.

I immediately called the commanding officers responsible for allocating manpower to the DPM and inquired about the absence of most of their officers at roll call. I was told that these Divisions and Bureaus, while assigned responsibility for the DPM on paper, were unable to send contingents due to other pressing needs. Having seen these "magic acts" before, I telephoned the Deputy Chief of the Patrol Bureau to discuss the matter. I "suggested" that, if these commanders refused to supply the necessary manpower, the deputy chief should cancel the DPM. I further related that District Three could address the issue of crime suppression with its own personnel.

I then set about establishing our District Three Area Saturation Patrol team. Within a very short period of time, the district's personnel not only eliminated the problem for which the DPM had been created, the ASP team had successfully addressed and reduced crime and disorder throughout the entire district, including the neighborhoods surrounding Marquette University, where panhandlers had discouraged economic development and harassed students. In fact, we did such a good job of discouraging panhandling in the Marquette University sector that the commanding officer of District One, which encompassed the geographical area directly to the east, complained that vagrants and other shakedown artists had been displaced within his district. Of course, this same commander did not have an initiative in place to discourage such conduct.

These were but a few examples from my district-level and tactical experiences—those that slowly evolved into the strategy that we began calling Area Saturation Patrol.

CHAPTER SIX

AREA SATURATION PATROL – DEFINED

ASP is a policing strategy which is designed to conduct on-going active patrols of Police District (neighborhood) crime hot spots. It addresses the concerns of the good people living and working in these neighborhoods with laser-like precision to liberate neighborhoods thereby greatly reducing the collateral damage of previous policing strategies designed to cast a web (aka: occupying neighborhoods) over an entire neighborhood. The ultimate goal is to create crime free neighborhoods in which good people can have a high quality of life free from the intimidation of thugs.

ASP Officers develop targets based on their day to day observations; neighborhood intelligence (informants as well as direct lines of communications with good people living and working in the various neighborhoods); and daily Crime Trend Analysis conducted by their Commanding Officer and his Community Liaison Officer(s).

The ASP unit is comprised of anywhere from 6 to 16 to 20 Officers and their assigned Sergeant who leads them on Street Sweeper Operations conducted no less than 3 times per week. This unit functions as a team and runs as a pack to include its own Patrol Prisoner Wagon. (Ideally, a team of Narcotics Detectives, Criminal Investigation Detectives, Juvenile Division Officers, Probation & Parole Officers, Neighborhood Services Division personnel, District Prosecutors, and any other personnel with responsibility to improve neighborhoods will accompany the ASPs on a Street Sweeper mission. These additional units will be "the tail on the kite", serve in a support capacity, and will not be actively engaged in the forward operations. Example: Probation/Parole will assist in checking out those in custody at a particular location and "violate" those who may be in violation of their probation/parole terms.)

ASP Officers must be in uniform. It is okay (and recommended) for them to ride in unmarked squads, but they must be highly visible upon alighting from their vehicles. This eliminates any confusion on the part of the bad guys as to who is approaching them and also gives the good people the high police visibility in their neighborhoods that they are demanding. *The uniform also eliminates any possibility of an ASP Officer being mistaken for a bad guy if a foot pursuit takes place and basic Officers respond. A plainclothes Officer can easily be mistaken for a bad guy and, if he has his gun drawn, may be shot by a friendly who mistakes him for the bad guy. (Plainclothes should only be used for surveillance purposes.)*

The number of ASP Officers must be sufficient to overwhelm the bad guys. In other words, if bad guys are congregating in groups of 6 to 8 or more, then the ASP Officers must be of sufficient manpower strength to outnumber and flank them. Requiring ASP Officers to have to resort to calling for additional help defeats the purpose and is counterproductive.

Enforcement of all City Ordinances and State Statutes is imperative if this mission is to accomplish its goal. (That is not to say there is no discretion, however all nuisance type violations must be addressed with the intent of immediate termination. For example, it defeats the purpose if a Public Drinker is cited and released; if an Aggressive Panhandler is cited and released; if a Public Urinator is cited and released.) The point is to do everything possible to rid neighborhoods of the very people who are constantly creating the demand for service and who are bringing down the quality of life as well as attracting or playing an active role in violent/property crimes in the neighborhood.

ASP operations must be flexible. Hours must be as needed to address varying concerns and to keep the bad guys off balance. Flexible hours will cause bad guys to never know when the ASPs will be in the neighborhoods and will leave bad guys with the impression that there are many more ASP Officers than actually exist.

CHAPTER SEVEN

NEIGHBORHOOD MEETINGS

District Three had many neighborhood organizations, and each sought to meet with me after I became the commander. Having prior knowledge of the district's issues from Compstat meetings, I was keenly aware that many community activists were unhappy with what they rightfully perceived as a lack of adequate enforcement by the MPD. I, therefore, elected to develop a policing strategy and enforcement philosophy prior to holding any initial meetings with neighborhood organizations. This, of course, was a different tact than I took in 1992 when I met with residents of District Two to inform them of the establishment of a DPM.

When the leaders of various groups in District Three called to schedule meetings, I explained that I had to get the house in order before dedicating the time to meet with them. My intention was to give each group an opportunity to see, first hand, the work our officers were doing. I did not want these meetings to devolve into the summer of 2001 pitchforks and torches affair, where a local newspaper displayed photographs of angry residents shaking their fingers at District Three's commanding officer during a community meeting.

Eventually, these meetings did come to fruition. One of the first occurred at the Master Lock Corporation, where the President of the Metcalfe Park Neighborhood Association, Larry Moore, introduced me by commenting that he had received a telephone call from Chief Arthur Jones explaining that I would be the new commander at District Three. Moore went on to tell those in attendance that he questioned Chief Jones' decision to replace an African-American captain with a white commander but, soon afterwards, had a change of heart when he noticed a visible increase in the number of officers patrolling the Metcalfe Park neighborhood.

One of the first things I did when speaking at a neighborhood-type gathering was to explain who I was and what my objectives were. I would begin by telling the audience that I was not Ronald McDonald; that these meetings were not about holding hands and singing "We Are The World"; that these meetings should serve as an impetus to exchange information with the ultimate goal being the reduction of crime and, therefore, an improvement in their neighborhood's quality-of-life.

On one occasion, I received a call from a business person in the district who requested that I sit on some type of neighborhood beautification board. I asked if crime problems were going to be discussed at these meetings. When she responded that crime was not a priority at these meetings, I declined the invitation by explaining that it was my responsibility to make neighborhoods safe and liberate the residents from intimidation of the thug element. Of course, I offered to attend any meeting where crime suppression was going to be a topic of discussion. Apparently that wasn't a concern of this woman as she never called back to invite me to any of her meetings. Nonetheless, reducing crime was my goal and I was committed to remain focused on making the district that I commanded a safe haven for the law-abiding.

In some instances, district captains actively participated in events, such as neighborhood clean-ups. A CO's participation sometimes included painting over graffiti and picking-up garbage strewn about in alleys and streets. I was a crime-fighter and did not see my responsibility as including the cleanup of these neighborhoods, so I did not participate in that endeavor although I did assign, and in some cases personally supervised, officers who escorted groups of concerned residents as they conducted their activities so that they would not be targeted and/or harassed by the criminal element. That was how I saw our law enforcement function.

When attending community meetings, I would bring all or at least some of our ASP officers and/or Squad officers along for the purpose of introducing them to the law abiding residents that they serve. These types of interactions build trust and open lines of communication needed to exchange intelligence. Since, my supervisory responsibilities included attending these meetings, I also felt it necessary to have street officers present so they could interact and hear the concerns of the community.

This gave residents an opportunity to put names with the faces of the officers they saw patrolling in their neighborhoods. These interactions also served as a catalyst for street officers to converse with neighborhood residents in a relaxed atmosphere free of interruptions.

Some officers took it upon themselves to exchange cell phone numbers with selected members of the community further opening regular lines of communication. These types of person-to-person contacts empowered ASP units and the community by enabling officers to respond to real time reports of criminal/nuisance activity. Ideally, these types of communications should occur between the community member and the ASP unit sergeant; however, when patrolling as a group with a supervisor, it is imperative that the sergeant be made aware of any/all such communications prior to an ASP unit response to a particular problem.

What we were doing was a little outside the norm, but such lines of communications and rapid response foster trust between the community and law enforcement. When problems are promptly addressed by the police the swift actions serve as a catalyst to report criminal activity. When frustrated residents feel that the police are too busy and cannot address matters in a timely manner, the pubic feels disenfranchised and soon looks the other way. If the attitude of a law enforcement agency is such that they only respond to major crimes, or if their response times to calls for service is slow, then people will assume that the police do not care and they will stop calling. Moreover, the criminal element will pick up on this and become increasingly emboldened.

An example of what I mean by how important it is to respond promptly to citizen concerns occurred in the summer of 2001 when I was the commanding officer of District Five. As it so happened, on this particular day the district had a Street Sweeper Operation in progress. A resident, who was conducting business inside the district station, observed me enter my office. He then asked one of the front desk personnel if he could speak with me. This resident explained that as he was leaving his residence a short time earlier he observed a group of young men causing a disturbance, which included driving cars on the sidewalk. He requested that I have a unit patrol the area in order to prevent this conduct from being repeated. As the man was sitting in my office, I telephoned Sgt. Bill Potterton, who was supervising the ASP unit's Street Sweeper Operation and asked Sgt. Potterton if he had any ASP squads in the area of this complaint. I then informed this resident that the problem would be addressed forthwith. In less than 30 minutes, Sgt. Potterton and the ASP team had several people in custody and the issue was resolved.

It is important to note that this resident was not in my office pounding his fist on the desk and demanding immediate action, although that is precisely what he received. This is the type of response a district-specific ASP operation provides. One can only imagine the satisfaction a citizen receives knowing that his or her concerns were promptly addressed.   With an ASP unit at a commanding officer's disposal, a dispatcher need not receive a call for service and then locate a squad to respond. Problems are addressed by officers empowered to expedite service in a timely fashion. Back in the day, old-school copper's had a saying for this: "You call, we haul."

One thing I learned after my first neighborhood meeting, held within the confines of District Five, is that there is a certain disconnect among the populous about the problems that occur in someone else's neighborhood. Human nature dictates that residents of a community are interested first and foremost with what transpires in their own backyards. I soon learned that it is bad practice to lump together various neighborhood meetings into one event. A large, omnibus-type meeting just doesn't work. Although attending individual neighborhood meetings was more time consuming, they were much more effective and established clearer lines of communication with residents.

Chapter Eight

Response to Dispatched Assignments

ASP Officers should not be dispatched to routine assignments for obvious reasons. To do so would undermine the overall purpose of the operation and render it ineffective. If, however, the backlog of assignments becomes too great, an arrangement should be made with the Communications Division C.O. that a Dispatcher supervisor can contact the District Shift C.O. and/or ASP Sergeant who will authorize one or several ASP Squads to handle assignments until the backlog is manageable or no longer exists.

It is imperative, though, that ASP officers respond to any major incidents that they are near and take whatever action is necessary. If their involvement results in an arrest, the ASP officers should become the primary investigators and file the appropriate reports. However, if no arrest is made (example: a false alarm; a suspect no longer on scene; etc.) then the patrol unit originally dispatched should handle the matter while the ASP officers return to their primary duties.

The ASP unit should also include at least two officers assigned to an auto theft squad. These officers should work closely with detectives who investigate vehicle thefts city-wide. The officers assigned to the auto theft squad will answer to their district captain and are responsible for investigating auto thefts, gathering intelligence on motor vehicle theft rings within the district, and sharing their findings with other ASP and patrol units. They too shall work flexible hours and not be dispatched to routine assignments.

BASIC PATROL UNITS VS. ASP UNITS

RESPONSIBILITIES & TEAM APPROACH

- Basic patrol units handle calls for service; thereby, freeing-up ASP personnel to perform their function of focusing on hotspots and specific problem people. (To use a football analogy: Basic Squads are like football linemen and ASP units are like running backs carrying the ball. If the linemen make their blocks, the backs score and the team wins the game.)

- Nothing herein prohibits Basic Squad Officers from exercising individual initiative in the mission to fight crime and make neighborhoods safer. When not responding to calls for service, or writing reports related thereto, Basic Squad Officers are expected to conduct traffic stops and Field Interviews along with their other patrol duties.

- Ideally, basic patrol units, with some exceptions, should be two-person squads to enhance effectiveness and for safety of the officers.

CHAPTER NINE

OTHER ADVANTAGES

One man patrol squads can function much more efficiently if they know that they will receive quick support from ASP teams when they call for backup. This means that an Officer working a one man squad, who observes suspicious activity in an alley or a group of thugs loitering, can lay back and call for help from the ASPs who will be available quickly to provide adequate support. Without the ASP operation, one man squads are much more likely to ignore such incidents or have to wait for a long period of time for backup – assuming the Dispatcher even allows them to wait or sends a backup unit.

ASP operations in each police district also offer the added advantage of being a "Rapid Deployment Force," readily available to respond to any crisis with a fairly sizeable number of officers. Utilizing the ASP units in this manner can address a need without reducing the level of service within a district or city-wide.

This strategy was employed in the summer of 2003 when Milwaukee's busiest geographical area, the MPD's District Seven, was experiencing a surge in violent crime in one particular neighborhood. The assistant police chief instructed District Five's commander, Captain Vince Flores, and me to deploy our ASP teams into District Seven to address the affected area. After approximately a week of intense patrol and strict enforcement the problem was resolved.

ASP teams must be assigned to respective Districts and must be under the Command of the District Captain. Anyone accompanying an ASP Street Sweeper Operation must also be under the Command of the District Captain. That includes Detectives and Narcotics personnel. The chain-of-command in an ASP operation needs to be direct to enhance maximum effectiveness and to hold a specific commander accountable for crime trends in his/her District and the resolution of same. This means that intelligence must be shared between those other Divisions/Bureaus working Street Sweeper Operations. That cooperation rarely occurred during my time with the DPM at District #2 as well as during my time as Lieutenant and especially as Captain of Districts #5 and #3 and is precisely why it is necessary for a police chief, or one of the chief's immediate subordinates, to regularly visit different districts and bureaus—announced or unannounced—to ensure that members of the police department are actively cooperating with each other.

CHAPTER TEN

OPERATION STREET SWEEPER RECEIVES A NATIONAL AWARD

The following is from a publication describing Operation Street Sweeper[xv] and our National Award from the United States Department of Justice - Executive Office of Weed and Seed awarded in 2002 for calendar 2001. The award received was one of only five such awards handed out across the country by the Department of Justice – Executive Office of Weed and Seed.

OPERATION STREET SWEEPER, MILWAUKEE WEED AND SEED, WISCONSIN

DESCRIPTION: Operation Street Sweeper brings the two "prongs" of the Weed and Seed strategy together to work with law enforcement and residents to reduce street drug dealing and crime in the community. In 2001, District Capt. Glenn Frankovis was assigned to the 5th District of the Milwaukee Police Department, which includes the Weed and Seed United South area. He made a strong commitment to reduce "hotspot" areas through Operation Street Sweeper. Milwaukee's bridge between community residents and law enforcement agencies is the Community Partners Program. The community partners work directly in the neighborhood to provide resource information about services and learn about residents' crime concerns. As the partners gain trust and credibility in the community, residents are more willing to assist the Milwaukee Police Department and other law enforcement entities (e.g., the Milwaukee High Intensity Drug Trafficking Area) and inform them about illegal activities in the community. Residents have responded positively to the police department's outreach, response, and improved interaction with the community. The program has already affected the neighborhood; residents observe "peaceful nights" and children can play outside because gunshots have stopped. Law enforcement also has benefited from the residents' positive feedback and cooperation.

GLENN D. FRANKOVIS

PARTNERS: Milwaukee Police Department--5th District; Milwaukee High Intensity Drug Trafficking Area; Community Partners Program, U.S. Attorney's Office for the Eastern District of Wisconsin." (A copy of the letter submitted by the U.S. Attorney's Office of the eastern district of Wisconsin, dated April 19, 2002, nominating Operation Street Sweeper for this award is located in the appendix of this book.)

Chapter Eleven

Quality-of-Life Policing and its Effects on Reducing Crime

1. Violent crime is committed primarily by thugs;

2. Thugs are not Monday thru Friday 9A to 5P type people;

3. Thugs loiter, drive defective autos, and generally engage in disorderly conduct; they also accumulate warrants;

4. Quality of Life policing, coupled with the development of good neighborhood intelligence, specifically targets these thugs by seeking them out and summarily arresting them for any and all ordinance and State Statute violations. It also stops them for any and all traffic violations which then allows cops to conduct wanted checks and, in most cases, search autos for weapons and contraband. It encourages cops to use the laws as a tool to make neighborhoods safe.

5. The development of good neighborhood intelligence greatly reduces the possibility of collateral damage - good people getting caught in the web. And in a District centric type deployment of police officers, as opposed to deploying them out of a central location - like a gang squad, the District officers know the good people from the bad people and develop a rapport as well as the kind of trust and confidence necessary to get the job done.

6. Since most major crimes are committed by thugs, many of whom also become homicide and shooting victims, policy makers should conclude that a no-nonsense quality-of-life policing strategy, as outlined above, will result in fewer homicides, shootings, and other violent offenses. A hard reality dictates that it is extremely difficult for the criminal element to work their will when they occupy jail cells, even for only four or five hours on municipal ordinance charges. When members of the anti-social, crime committing subculture spend a few Friday or Saturday nights inside a cell, they sometimes get that 'come to Jesus' moment or go elsewhere to commit their crimes. This occurred on a micro-level when I commanded

District Three. The same results can be accomplished city-wide if implemented properly.

7. When members of the criminal element are in jail, even for minor violations, calls for police service should decrease. As a result, officers will have more time to patrol their squad areas and protect the law-abiding. This will also eliminate the practice of inter-district dispatching, which involves moving street officers on patrol from one area of the city to another during peak periods of demand.

8. A District Area Saturation Patrol (ASP) Unit for each Police District needs to be put in place to allow District Captains the flexibility of deploying a "strike force" sufficiently manned and capable of using neighborhood intelligence obtained from regular meetings and anonymous tips to identify and arrest the drug dealers/users and others who are intimidating the good people in these various neighborhoods. District Captains can then be held accountable for crime in their Police Districts.

RESULTS:

These are the statistics provided to me by the Milwaukee Police Department during my time as Captain of District #3 (November 2001 to December 2003):

HOMICIDES:

- Calendar 2001: 35
- Calendar 2002: 18
- **Decrease: 48.6%**
- Calendar 2003: 30*

* 28 actual in 2003 plus 2 cleared in 2003 which occurred in the 1980s and were put in the 2003 count) (We experienced 6 homicides in April and 6 in May, many of which were due to a drug dealer we knew who had Chicago connections and lived in the area of 27th and Clarke.) (Several of those 2003 homicides were domestic violence and infant homicides.

Homicides in the Metcalfe Park Neighborhood:
an area seemingly out of control in 2001

- 2001: 09
- 2002: 03
- 2003: 04

ROBBERIES:

- 2001: 632
- 2002: 625
- **Decrease: 1.1%**
- 2003: 491
- **Decrease: 21.7%**

BURGLARIES:

- 2001: 1166
- 2002: 962
- **Decrease: 17.5%**
- 2003: 868
- **Decrease: 11.1%**

FORCIBLE SEX OFFENSES:

- ➢ 2001: 199
- ➢ 2002: 160
- ➢ **Decrease: 19.6%**
- ➢ 2003: 153
- ➢ **Decrease: 7.3%**

AGGRAVATED ASSAULT:

- ➢ 2001: 992
- ➢ 2002: 811
- ➢ **Decrease: 18.2%**
- ➢ 2003: 701
- ➢ **Decrease: 14.4%**

THEFT:

- ➢ 2001: 4126
- ➢ 2002: 3868
- ➢ **Decrease: 6.3%**
- ➢ 2003: 3837
- ➢ **Decrease: 2.5%**

MOTOR VEHICLE THEFT:

- ➢ 2001: 1254
- ➢ 2002: 1279
- ➢ **Increase: 2.0%**
- ➢ 2003: 1228
- ➢ **Decrease: 4.1%**

SHOOTINGS:

- ➢ 2001: 187
- ➢ 2002: 107
- ➢ **Decrease: 42.8%**
- ➢ 2003: 112

Overall reduction in Part 1 crimes for 2002 was 8.1%. The 8.1% reduction in Part 1 crimes was the best reduction for the 7 Districts of the MPD.

Overall reduction in Part 1 crimes for 2003 was 6.5%.

Reported violent crime in 2003 vs 2002 was DOWN 15.5%. This was the best reduction for the 7 Police Districts of MPD.

According to statistics released by the FBI's Uniform Crime Reporting Program (UCR) in its annual publication Crime in the United States...the estimated volume of violent crime in the United States declined 3 percent from the 2002 figure.

Collectively, U.S. cities experienced a 3.0% decrease in violent crime compared to 2002. - Source: (FBI Law Enforcement Bulletin of April 2005 - page 9)

Although the media tends to hype the number of murders per year as a benchmark to ascertain the rate of violent crime, as well as to judge the effectiveness of a police department's crime fighting strategy, I firmly believe that more focus should be given to three major crime categories:

Aggravated Batteries

Robberies (Armed & Unarmed)

Shootings (to include shots fired at people and/or property)

This is not to diminish the tragedy of a homicide; however, some murders are beyond the ability of law enforcement to prevent. Deaths related to domestic violence and shaken baby syndrome, for example, generally occur in the confines of private abodes protected by the Fourth Amendment. No patrol strategy that I am aware of can prevent what transpires inside the residence unless a neighbor hears or sees something suspicious, or a Terry[16] stop results in the apprehension of a suspect on his or her way to commit a crime.

The three major crime categories (Aggravated Battery; Robberies; and Shootings) that I used to determine the success or failure of our policing strategy and deployment of Officers are primarily street type crimes that can impact on anyone in any neighborhood thereby greatly reducing the Quality of Life in that neighborhood and the fear of becoming a random victim. That is not to say that one cannot be victimized in any given neighborhood, but the effectiveness of our policing strategies can be judged more accurately by whether or not street crime is increasing or decreasing. Moreover, perceptions of street-level crime can impact the economic development of an entire area.

Of course, the best factor in determining our effectiveness in any given neighborhood is still the feedback we get from the people who live and work in that neighborhood. One has only to put himself in the place of the residents in these neighborhoods to understand that.

CHAPTER TWELVE

SELECTION OF SUPERVISORS AND OFFICERS

All aspects of the Area Saturation Patrol concept are important, but perhaps the most significant is the selection of the sergeant who will lead the team. I had the luxury, and good fortune, of having two such individuals assigned to my command at Districts Five and Three.

Sgt. William Potterton led our District Five ASP team. He was directly responsible for the creation of the tactical crime fighting operation known as Operation Street Sweeper, which was initiated in the early summer of 2001. Up to that time, our ASP units worked from 4 pm. – 12 midnight and did not patrol, on a regular basis, as a group.

One of our two district-level community prosecutors, Derek Mosley (currently a City of Milwaukee Municipal Judge), came to my office with a request. He told me that during one of his meetings with members of a group representing a neighborhood within the district, he was told that the criminal element had recognized that our ASP units typically patrolled between 4PM and Midnight. Assistant District Attorney Mosley asked if our team could, on occasion, alter their hours. I replied that we would do so and asked ADA Mosley to consult with Sgt. Potterton to formulate a plan of action.

Sgt. Potterton quickly assessed the problem and came to me with his written plan which he called Operation Street Sweeper. I authorized the plan and it was implemented with great success. Sgt. Potterton's after-action reports, which contained the statistical results, including arrests, weapons recovered, drugs recovered, etc., for the first several operations exceeded my expectations.

When I forwarded these after-action reports, with my cover report, to Milwaukee Police Chief Arthur Jones, he ordered all district commanders to commence their own district-wide Street Sweeper operations.

In November of 2001, I was transferred to District Three by Chief Jones; whereupon, I immediately took steps to organize an Area Saturation Patrol team. Fortunately, I was able to arrange for the transfer of Sgt. Chris Brown—a savvy, street-level supervisor that I had served with as a lieutenant at another work location. Sgt. Brown hit the ground running and organized a team of ASP officers, which later expanded over a two-year period.

No one, including myself, thought that we could turn things around in short order; however, in less than 6 months the ASP team and other officers assigned to the district had restored order to previously out-of-control neighborhoods. The impetus to get the job done was Operation Street Sweeper (almost daily at this time), coupled with a very strict, no nonsense philosophy of law enforcement. Violations resulted in summary arrests, which meant a conveyance to jail.

No doubt, a large part of this success was attributed to community involvement, which enabled District Three ASP units to focus on the criminal element. The trust-based policing model—a bond that formed between District Three personnel and the residents of the community—was akin to the trust-and-confidence model implemented by the military during our efforts to liberate Iraq and Afghanistan. These residents lived in the affected neighborhoods 24/7 and, as such, became our eyes and ears. With their help we were able to conduct Street Sweeper operations with surgical precision; thereby, reducing the likelihood of collateral damage, such as stopping and detaining persons not involved in criminal activity.

Along with the help of the residents, daily Crime Trend Analysis (CTA), conducted by District Three Community Liaison Officer Tom Kupsik and myself, quickly identified crime trends and empowered ASP unit supervisors to redeploy resources as needed. This was time consuming work; however, these CTA's paid tremendous dividends in the form of reduced crime and resulted in some very satisfied customers — residents whose neighborhoods were finally receiving the kind of attention required to improve their quality-of-life.

One of the things that actually surprised me was the small number of complaints generated by Operation Street Sweeper. Of the handful that did trickle in, virtually none had any merit, which was proof positive that an aggressive, yet precise, policing operation—staffed by law enforcement professionals—can reduce crime without increasing tensions in the community.

CHAPTER THIRTEEN

DISTRICT COMMANDER'S RESPONSIBILITIES

Crime Trend Analysis must be done daily and include, but not be limited to, the following:

You must immerse yourself in your District/Precinct. That means you must be more informed about the crime in your District and ahead of the curve on crime trends than the people who preside over your Crime Analysis Meetings.

Review of all Arrest Reports generated in his District/Precinct for the purpose of determining who is committing the crimes; where they live; what areas of the Districts the crimes are being committed and when; what crimes are being committed; which Officers are making the arrests & how they made the arrest (strategy/techniques).

Information from the Shift Commander's Log Book

Review Daily Major Crime Summaries sent to the District by the Detective Bureau or Crime Analysis Section.

Attend Neighborhood Meetings for the purpose of communicating strategy (limited to what we're going to do without compromising the operation) and philosophy (which helps build trust & confidence leading to the establishment of lines of communication and real time intelligence information). When the subject of

Our Crime Analysis meetings were held once a week on Wednesdays in the afternoon. The crimes and trends discussed consisted of those which occurred the previous week, therefore we were not actually discussing the latest crimes and crime trends. Essentially, a crime trend from last week might already have been stopped with an arrest and a new crime trend was in the making. I viewed this as a flaw in the process and came prepared to discuss the past week as well as crimes and crime trends which I had identified up to 11 o'clock the morning of the Crime Analysis meeting. I was also prepared to explain our deployment strategy to address and snuff out any recent crime trend that we had identified.

crime stats comes up, it is imperative to acknowledge that crime trends may be down, however a 10% drop in Burglaries is just a number to those who have been victimized by Burglary or other crimes where percentages indicate a downward trend. Save your chest thumping for the weekly Crime Analysis Meetings with your bosses.

LIVE THE PROGRAM

Must take personal responsibility and care about the neighborhoods in his/her District/Precinct (meaning police it as if he/she lived in these neighborhoods; take an attitude of "If it's significant to you, then it's significant to me" when people bring problems to his/her attention). No problem is too small (Broken Windows Theory of Policing). If you tend to the brush fires, you may not have to deal with a major forest fire.

ONLY BANK IN TOWN ATTITUDE

This means that people depend on us to do our jobs. They don't have any other legal option. They can't take their concerns elsewhere, so it is imperative that we listen to them and take action to address their concerns.

COMMANDERS NEED THE TRUST OF THE COMMUNITY

This requires building confidence by providing services in a timely manner. If a commander promises to address a problem, it is important to follow through. Commanders should take a results oriented attitude and resolve quality-of-life issues the same manner they would expect them to be dealt with in their own neighborhood.

Chapter Fourteen

The Importance of Decentralized, District Operations vs. Centralized Operations

GREATLY REDUCES ANIMOSITY

There is always that internal infighting and/or indifference between district officers and those assigned to centralized specialty units, such as tactical or gang units. Keeping an ASP unit district-specific reduces the likelihood of conflict, as the officers all know one another and there is a much greater opportunity and tendency to share information and work as a team.

AN INCENTIVE FOR OFFICERS WHO ARE MOTIVATED TO BECOME PART OF SUCH A SPECIALIZED UNIT.

Officers assigned to standard patrol, who have a desire to work on the ASP units, will strive to earn consideration for such an assignment. Individual characteristics, such as a willingness to work as a team; demonstrating one's ability to think on their feet; and establishing command presence, are important requirements for consideration;

Allows the ASP sergeant and the commanding officer to observe and select only the best candidates for assignments to ASP units.

KEEPS AN OPERATION CLOSE TO HOME

Decentralized units of government, including those within police departments, are more efficient and attune to the problems within their geographical areas of responsibility. ASP officers' knowledge of an area and its residents will greatly reduce collateral damage.

ALLOWS A DISTRICT COMMANDER TO ADDRESS SMALL AND MAJOR ISSUES

ASP units give commanding officers the flexibility to deploy their own resources rather than relying on assistance from other centralized divisions, whose personnel may not be available when a problem presents itself.

A centrally located gang intelligence unit, consisting of detectives who compile information from internal and external sources, and communicate daily with district commanders and ASP personnel, should keep tabs on suspects committing crimes in various police districts. Members of the centralized gang unit should be responsible for prisoner interviews when appropriate.

CHAPTER FIFTEEN

PREEMPTIVE POLICING VS. REACTIVE POLICING

Preemptive Policing is a term that I use to describe a style of policing that I first observed in the early part of my career at District Five. At the time, in the minds of hard-charging cops, District Five was the place to be. The officers and supervisors who served there took a great deal of pride in working in some of the busiest, most violent neighborhoods of Milwaukee.

> When police officers actually have unobligated patrol time, meaning they are not answering dispatched calls for service, a concerted effort should be made to exercise individual initiative to prevent future calls from ever occurring.

Although not every incident resulted in an arrest, the officers I worked with weren't shy about applying a set of handcuffs when a summary arrest was the best solution to resolving a problem. This included City of Milwaukee Ordinance violations and certain traffic violations, when the identity of the driver was in question. Aggressive policing included field Interviews and traffic stops for "minor violations," such as defective tail lamps, non-functioning license plate lamps, and hood ornaments that displayed lights other than authorized by state statute. Many of these stops resulted in arrests for open warrants, drug trafficking charges, and weapons violations.

Retired FBI Agent Dr. Roger H. Davis mentioned similar proactive policing tactics in an article entitled, *Cruising for Trouble: Gang-Related Drive-By Shootings*, in the January 1995 *FBI Law Enforcement Bulletin*.[17]

"If a community's problem is identified as youths with access to illegal guns," Davis wrote, "an aggressive program should be devised to take their guns and to provide alternatives for the excitement they seek. Such a program may include aggressive field stops and focused vehicle and residence searches to reduce the risk of shooting incidents."

An example is a traffic stop I conducted at 3:00 a.m. while a street supervisor in District Two on July 4th, 1982. I initiated the stop after I observed a vehicle travelling the wrong way on a one-way street. When making traffic stops, I generally remained at my squad with the door open and stood behind the open door, with my gun in hand, so the operator of the vehicle could not observe the weapon. When circumstances dictated, I would shout directions and instruct the driver to exit his vehicle with a driver's license in hand, ruled permissible in the U.S. Supreme Court Decision, Pennsylvania v. Mimms 434 U.S. 106 (1977). When drivers complied, I would verbally order drivers to walk toward me and then to the sidewalk or curb area. In most cases, after determining that weapons were not present, I would holster my weapon; leave my position of cover; and then escort the driver to the sidewalk, where I would state the reason(s) for the stop. I would then permit a driver to return to the vehicle after the area around the driver's seat was searched for weapons. If I wasn't able to check the seat area for weapons, I would repeat the process when issuing a citation or warning.

In this particular case, because there were multiple occupants and because I did not yet have backup on scene, I instructed the driver to return to his vehicle and standby. While running a wanted check and driver information, I observed all of the occupants of the vehicle exit the vehicle and sit down on the walk area. This was very unusual conduct. When backup arrived, I instructed the officer to monitor the suspects while I searched the interior of the car. Looking inside the open driver's door, I observed bullets in plain view on the floorboard. I then instructed the back-up officer to hold the suspects at gunpoint. Searching further, I recovered multiple weapons—a .25 caliber semi-auto handgun, a 9mm semi-auto handgun, a .38 caliber revolver, and a knife. The driver and the occupants were all males from Chicago. It was learned later that one of the men had previously been deported for drug dealing and had returned to the U.S. illegally.

Detectives questioned the men but were unable to ascertain much information about the intent of those who had occupied the vehicle that night. It was safe to assume that they probably hadn't armed themselves for a tour of the sights of Milwaukee. In all likelihood, this simple traffic stop prevented a serious crime from occurring that night.

What doesn't get tabulated, and isn't apparent to anyone but street officers in the know, are the number of crimes that are prevented when police officers execute traffic stops and effect arrests for the "small things" that George Kelling and James Q. Wilson wrote about in *Broken Windows Theory*[18] which later became the crime fighting doctrine instituted by New York City Mayor Rudy Giuliani and the Commissioner of the NYPD, William Bratton. *Broken Windows* became the crime fighting model employed by many big city Police Departments in the mid-1990s. A form of this philosophy was later brought to Milwaukee's Police Department in 1996, when then Mayor John Norquist's Fire and Police Commission appointed Arthur Jones to the rank of Chief-of-Police. Ironically, Chief Jones and I both had worked at District Five during the same period in the 1970s.

Certainly, it isn't difficult to fathom that a field interview or a traffic stop might also prevent a robbery or some other type of violent crime from occurring. The arrests of those armed men in the vehicle I stopped, no doubt, made some neighborhood safer, even though those who might have been in harm's way most likely had no way of knowing that. The arrests and seizure of the firearms probably meant one less call to the police for a major incident investigation.

Because lives hang in the balance, police departments cannot afford to address issues in the same manner that fire departments do. Firefighters play defense and almost exclusively respond to events that are self-evident. When firefighters have "down time" their duties may consist of equipment maintenance or other such non-emergency functions. When police officers actually have unobligated patrol time, meaning they are not answering dispatched calls for service, a concerted effort should be made to exercise individual initiative to prevent future calls from ever occurring. Examples would be checking businesses to prevent burglaries or robberies; conducting Field Interviews of persons engaged in suspicious activity or who may match the description of suspects wanted for various offenses;

conducting traffic stops for violations of the traffic code; etc. Hence, the term "preemptive policing".

> REACTIVE POLICING IS LIKE A DOG CHASING ITS TAIL.

The crime occurs; law enforcement responds; a report is taken; and maybe an arrest is made. If the crime is not soon solved with an arrest, a neighborhood crime trend might begin. Residents might soon accuse the police of doing little to address crime and disorder. When this occurs, the police often get defensive; relations between law enforcement and the community deteriorate; and, if response times to calls for service lag, the perception becomes that the police are either inept or aloof. In reality though, when crime occurs, no matter how fast law enforcement responds, the crime has already happened and another victim asks, "Where are the cops when you need them?"

Chapter Sixteen

Take the Job Seriously

Ever hear the phrase "Don't take this job too seriously"? I used to hear it from some guys in my early days. In some cases it was said as a warning to prevent the stress associated with caring too much, and in other cases it was used as an excuse to do as little as possible. I was one of those lawmen who viewed my job as a calling. That's not to say I considered myself a great cop. I was fortunate enough to have worked among some of the truly great cops and supervisors in the Department during my career and learned much from them. My policing strategies and philosophy were built on the foundation they laid, and much of my success can be attributed to them.

There were many examples of why I believed the function of a lawman was to stand between thugs and good people, but this one stands out in my mind:

During one evening shift, while supervising the MPD's Tactical Enforcement Unit (TEU), Sgt. Fred Shippee and I responded with district-level patrol officers, as well as a handful of TEU units, to a call of "shots fired" in a residential area on Milwaukee's north side. Upon our arrival, those responsible for discharging weapons were gone; however, the smoke from the gunfire was still in the air and the expended shell casings were strewn about the street. It was another night of Milwaukee's version of *The Gunfight at the O.K. Corral,* except, unlike the movie, bodies did not litter the street. Unfortunately, as is often the case with these clowns, the perpetrators sprayed everything but their intended targets.

Upon checking residences for bullet holes and injured occupants, I was summoned by a man who wanted me to accompany him back to his house to see evidence of the gunfire. He took me upstairs to his daughter's bedroom to show me a bullet hole in her window facing the street. By the Grace of God, his daughter was not in the room at the time of the shooting. Had she been in her room, she might have looked out the window out of curiosity and been injured or killed by that stray round.

Having small kids of my own, I could empathize with this man and was furious that the punks would have absolutely no concern for others when settling their differences in the street. It was apparent to me that a different kind of policing strategy was going to be necessary to combat the problem. If these punks were going to roam the streets like packs of dogs, then our Officers were going to have to adopt that concept as well.

Unfortunately, as a street-level supervisor, I was not in a position to set policy or implement a strategy that would ultimately change the status quo of the MPD. On the other hand, having seen those killed in the streets, as well as the collateral damage emanating from stray gunfire, I took a deep, caring interest in those innocent bystanders who had been killed as well as their families; those who survived gunshot wounds; and the young children who, because of these senseless acts of violence, too often had to live in fear in what was supposed to be the most carefree years of their lives. When contemplating a policing strategy that would make a difference, I kept these memories in mind for future reference. Somewhere along the way I hoped a time might come when I could enact the changes needed to alter the status quo and diminish the perpetual cycle of violence.

This opportunity came much earlier than I anticipated. After leaving TEU for a day shift sergeant's position at District Two, on Milwaukee's near south side, I had the privilege to serve under the command of Captain David Bartholomew, a man who wasn't afraid to address problems and violent criminal activity (See the aforementioned DPM section in Chapter One).

As stated earlier, I did not consider myself an outstanding officer; however, I was able to identify good cops—those with the intelligence, the right attitude, and the work ethic required to fight and suppress crime. I also recognized that not all cops were the same. Some wanted to run and gun, and others just wanted to take assignments and conduct their investigations, and still others were incapable of doing either.

I decided it would be necessary to find ways to play the cards I was dealt. Coach Knight, who had learned from his mentors, said it this way:

"Again referring to Claire Bee: "It was one illustration of his advice that I heard more than once and can still hear today: make sure your best players are in their absolute best roles. Then use your supplementary players in just that, supplementary roles...."[19]

Of course, great cops working as a team require great leadership, and having had the good fortune to have worked for and among some great bosses I was able to identify what I needed to finish the puzzle and establish the ASP teams necessary to accomplish the mission of reducing crime in the Districts I Commanded and/or supervised.

As the commanding officer at Districts Five and Three, along with my other responsibilities, my role was to run interference with police managers who felt threatened by change or those who practiced—with little concern for the plight of crime victims—unbridled political correctness. This not only included dealing with some tentative administrators at police headquarters, but also a few district commanders, who knew nothing about ASP operations but were foolishly, and without merit, overly concerned about the civil rights of the criminal element. Not surprisingly, a small but vocal number of officers and supervisors at the district level—those who didn't want to work as hard as I demanded—tried to erect various barriers that supported the status quo of going-along to get-along. Needless to say, belonging to this good old boys' network wasn't a part of my DNA nor was complacency my idea of leadership.

Fortunately, for me, Chief Arthur Jones thought highly of the results derived by the hard work of my ASP units at Districts Five and Three. Jones championed these endeavors and, by doing so, made district-level policing more efficient and effective, while reducing crime and improving the quality-of-life for those who resided in troubled neighborhoods.

CHAPTER SEVENTEEN

LEADERSHIP

Throughout this book, I have given personal examples of what I believe to be outstanding leadership. Leadership, as concisely defined by Warren Bennis & Burt Nanus in their book, <u>Leaders: The Strategies for Taking Charge</u>[20], "Managers do things right; Leaders do the right thing."

I firmly believe that leadership is a quality that embodies solid decision making capabilities. It is imperative, though, that decision makers must not be afraid to fail.

> "A good solution applied with vigor now is better than a perfect solution applied ten minutes later."
> -- *General George S. Patton, Jr.*

In too many instances, vacillation is a character trait exhibited by law enforcement executives afraid to upset the apple cart. We have all been on thoroughfares controlled by four-way stop signs and watched as drivers experience a deer-in-the-headlights moment. I have observed this form of decision making paralysis in police work, too. A real leader knows that his/her decisions may not always work effectively. Yet, in too many instances, some law enforcement managers are unwilling to make a decision or take even the slightest risk for fear of being criticized. Ironically, these so-called executives will be the first to disparage the failures of those willing to grab the proverbial bull by the horns. Theodore Roosevelt identified these armchair quarterbacks as "timid souls who know neither victory nor defeat."

"But 'not afraid to lose' means to me that you're willing to do what you think has to be done to win," wrote Bobby Knight, "even if it deviates from the norm – even if it puts you out on the limb for criticism because it deviates from what the consensus thinks has to be done."[21]

It's also important to remember that there's a downside to not being satisfied. You must be capable of taking time to enjoy success. You can also become so intent on the 100% factor that you forget others have different levels of 100% - some levels are greater than yours and other levels not as great. It is the individual's 100% that you need to be satisfied with.

Using a sports analogy, if those under a leader's command are leaving 'everything on the field,' then, regardless of their strengths and weaknesses, these employees have given 100 percent. This is not to say that exceptional employees—those whose skill-sets are head-and-shoulders above the rest—are continuously giving 100 percent. Some personnel are aware that they are capable of doing more and need to be reminded of that occasionally. That being said leaders can become obsessed with high expectations and need to recognize when to loosen the reins.

Good leaders recognize that every individual is different; that each employee has their own dynamic to deal with at home; and that one's profession is just one facet, albeit important, of life. Good leaders understand the totality of prolonged stress. Human beings, overwhelmed by periods of unbearable pressures, are statistically likely to stumble in both their professional and personal lives. While executives cannot control external stressors, they do have some ability to minimize internal factors. Big-city policing is an incredibly stressful endeavor. Officers experience the worst of society on a daily basis. Sometimes, even the hardest-chargers require a needed respite in order to maintain their sanity.

A chief-of-police worthy of his or her rank appreciates subordinates who think outside the box. Innovative thinking and the ability to remain one-step ahead of the criminal element are attributes that contribute to crime reduction and improve the quality-of-life for those who abide by and respect the law. Adequate preparation also enhances the likelihood of success; should result in a decrease in the use of force by police officers; and should minimize the number of citizen complaints. Crime reduction creates a safe environment and encourages economic development; thereby, increasing opportunities for employment while expanding the tax base.

On the subject of crime reduction, in his book *Leadership*, former New York Mayor Rudy Giuliani, wrote:

"We attacked crime immediately, but we knew that it would take time to show results. And reducing the number of crimes wouldn't be enough: people had to see an improvement, not just hear about it. If crime went down but the existing amount of pushing and shoving, urinating on the streets, and other quality-of-life issues remained the same, we would never have a convincing case that life was better. We had to get people to be safe and to feel safe."[22]

In its totality, the success of these types of proactive policing strategies abound. The proactive concept of patrol worked wonders in District Five, where I was assigned as an Officer, lieutenant and, later, as a captain. The ASP philosophy of policing doesn't take a PhD to understand, although it does entail the deployment of dedicated and ethical law enforcement personnel—those who care, view police work as a calling, and are intent on making a difference.

To make this point, one might want to walk-a-mile in the shoes of a resident living in a decaying neighborhood. Each day, groups of thugs and other dregs of society diminish their quality-of-life by selling drugs, "bumpin'" their cars' musical amplification systems, and intimidating others who dare walk down the street. Experienced law enforcement officers know that good people living in such neighborhoods are often fearful of getting involved. After all, a real possibility exists that the criminal element might retaliate with deadly force.

Thug organizations, such as the Outlaws Motorcycle Club and the Hells Angels, have no qualms about putting the populace on notice. In 2001, after federal indictments were handed down, members of the Outlaws MC sported t-shirts that read, "Snitches are a dying breed." The Hells Angels, the world's largest one-percenter organization, infamously boasts that "three men can keep a secret if two are dead." In Milwaukee's central city, a 'no snitch' mentality has crept into the body fabric. As a result, residents of troubled neighborhoods will call to report suspicious and/or criminal activity while seeking to remain anonymous. Without a complainant or a willing witness, the task of establishing a reasonable suspicion for a stop or the probable cause required to effect an arrest is sometimes problematic. However, if officers arrive in short order and witness an offense, the need for witnesses is moot.

For example, should a resident call to report an intoxicated person, standing on the corner drinking from a 40 ounce bottle of beer and harassing passersby, and officers witness the incident of public drinking, action can be taken without a complainant. This is where trust and confidence enter the equation.

In this situation, three scenarios will likely play out:

The officers observe a public drinking violation and simply "advise" the violator to "move along." The Officers then drive-off leaving the problem to fester – perhaps the perpetrator walks around the corner and continues the disruptive conduct.

The officers arrive and observe the violation. They issue a non-summary civil forfeiture citation to the offender. The officers once again drive-off without resolving the pattern of disorder.

The officers arrive on scene and observe the violation. They summarily arrest the violator, search the perpetrator incident to a lawful arrest, place the suspect in their squad car, and convey the offender to the district station, where they issue a citation. The officers then go back in-service. The district's shift commander then determines whether or not to immediately release the offender from the district station or have the perpetrator conveyed downtown to be booked.

In the first scenario the resident is peeking between their blinds and watches as the officers essentially do nothing to resolve the matter. Hence, the caller loses confidence that the police actually care and decides that it is fruitless to contact law enforcement.

In the second scenario, the caller draws the same conclusion, as the police respond and take an action akin to a slap on the wrist, but, in reality, do nothing to discontinue the pattern of disorder.

In the third scenario, however, the caller observes that the police have taken action to remove and resolve the problem. The resident is, therefore, empowered by the police response and now believes that their concerns will be addressed and their involvement, even if done anonymously, can and will make a difference. This resident will likely call again when a problem presents itself and will communicate their positive experiences about the police department's willingness to remove offenders in short order.

Of course the argument can be made that police are too busy to effect summary arrests for *minor* violations or that officers need to use *discretion*. Some police managers will claim that their officers cannot and should not arrest individuals for 'every little thing.' Then again, ask yourself: if a similar incident occurred on a corner near your home, would this type of conduct affect the neighborhood's quality-of-life? The Broken Windows Theory of policing does not mandate that every individual who commits an ordinance violation be summarily arrested. Broken Windows policing does, however, emphasize tending to minor issues so that they do not fester and become larger problems. I maintain that the summary arrest in the aforementioned scenario discourages the unacceptable conduct and sends a message to offenders that misconduct will not be taken lightly while sending an even more important message to the decent folk living in the neighborhood that the police care and will take action to make their Quality of Life better.

BACK TO LEADERSHIP

In the past, I have used the analogy of an outstanding baseball pitcher when discussing the characteristics of a great cop. Hall of Fame pitchers do not become great by grooving the ball down the center of the plate in order to make the strike call easy for the home plate umpire. Instead, good pitchers work the corners. In law enforcement, however, "working the corners" is looked upon by some managers as running rogue. Occasionally, a major league pitcher will throw a pitch outside the strike zone. Such a pitch might be a mistaken opportunity to hit the catchers target or might be done in the hopes that a hitter will swing at a pitch out of the strike zone. A good law enforcement officer—one who isn't afraid to make decisions—will make mistakes, but, similar to a major league pitcher, the law enforcement officer will not be wrong often. From my perspective, in the rare instances that it does occur, I would rather have officers lose a case at a motion hearing in court than simply sit on their hands because they are afraid to act. Even Hall of Fame pitchers, such as Sandy Koufax and Bob Gibson, sometimes served-up pitches that were knocked out of the park. No one, not even the greatest pitcher of all-time, is perfect.

When law enforcement administrators throw their officers under the proverbial bus for making a mistake in the heat of the moment, the message to the rank-and-file is crystal clear: risking one's life or career to police proactively while thinking outside the box is taboo. This type of reaction from law enforcement administrators usually materializes when the media or some politician target an officer or the police department in order to win awards or to gain favor with those who dislike authority. Trust is a big part of being a law enforcement officer. Conversely when police officers do not trust the members of the community that they serve, or worse the people they work for, crime and disorder will fester. I would much rather have officers under my command who, on occasion, need the reins pulled-in than officers who constantly require a figurative kick in the ass as motivation.

Others might disagree, but I believe that at no time is the job of being a law enforcement officer more dangerous than when cops in the field do not trust their administration to support them when their performance comes under fire from the media or the political class. Law enforcement administrators who succumb to armchair cops in newsrooms and at city hall are, quite frankly, too consumed with their own ambitions than they are about fighting crime. I have observed weak-kneed police administrators throw good officers under the bus too many times during my career and, quite frankly, I find it disgusting.

"In war, there is no substitute for victory, said General Douglas MacArthur, during his April 19, 1951, address to Congress. The general's words also apply to the war on crime. It is imperative that law enforcement and members of the community do everything possible to make cities and neighborhoods safer and inhospitable for the thug element.

The Area Saturation Patrol concept isn't some flavor of the day policing strategy that so often emanates from the lips of those in academia or elite think tanks. Policing is serious business. Real lives are involved, and good people depend on law enforcement to protect them, which is precisely why taxpayers generously fork over billions of dollars a year in the name of public safety.

"A GOOD SOLUTION APPLIED WITH VIGOR NOW IS BETTER THAN A PERFECT SOLUTION APPLIED TEN MINUTES LATER." -- *GENERAL GEORGE S. PATTON, JR.*

"I was probably a lot more happy-go-lucky before Vietnam than after and that's because I came to understand that carelessness and negligence and lousy leadership and self-serving officers and generals cost human lives", General H. Norman Schwarzkopf, told 20-20's Barbara Walters in 1991. "And you just can't forgive that. You cannot forgive that sort of crassness. People who are more concerned with their ambition than they are with their troops is unforgiveable to me and you know - and again, you're supposed to be able to forgive everything. I can't forgive that. I cannot forgive that."

"...some of the best leadership lessons I have ever learned have been taught by dumb officers, absolutely morally bankrupt officers who had no redeeming qualities, Schwarzkopf later explained. "In many cases, you learn far more from negative leadership than from positive leadership because you learn how not to do it."

In his book, *The Crime Fighter: How You Can Make Your Community Crime-Free*, former NYPD Deputy Commissioner Jack Maple notes several qualities, some of which I have addressed, that are necessary for effective crime fighting:

- "The City's highest elected official must have the political will to shake-up the police department and to stand firm if assertive but honorable police enforcement tactics come under fire. The mayor also must be self-confident enough to choose a police leader who may, due to talent and the nature of the work, eclipse the mayor in public approval ratings."

- "The leader of the police department must have a vision, must articulate it, and must repeat the message over and over again in both internal communications and through the press. The message must be direct and concise, communicating that the police department's primary objective is fewer victims of crime, and everything the department does will be directed toward and valued according to its contribution toward achieving that objective."

- "Benchmark goals should be set regularly, such as reducing violent crime rates to 1960 levels within two years. The leader must anticipate obstacles to achieving the goal and have the intestinal fortitude to overcome them. If there are no obstacles, the vision isn't one worth having, because it is an endorsement of doing business as usual."

- "The leader must lead from the front – exposing him or her to the same dangers and hardships as the cops in the field while monitoring whether the department's tactics and strategies are being carried out and whether or not they're working."

- "The leader must back the cops when they're right, train them when they make mistakes despite good intentions, and hang them when they betray the public's trust."

- "The leader must choose subordinate commanders who are confident and audacious and who, because they believe in the leader's vision, are able to extend the leader's vision of the entire field. The subordinate commanders must demonstrate by their presence that the department is an organization open to talent and they too must lead from the front. Subordinate commanders must be held accountable for the reduction of crime within their commands, and they should be capable of synchronizing the efforts of various operational units so that authority over patrol, narcotics, and detectives can be vested at the precinct or district level."

"Our society, at the present time," said Vince Lombardi, the head coach of the Green Bay Packers during a speech in the late 1960s, "seems to have sympathy only for the misfit, the ne'er-do-well, the maladjusted, the criminal, the loser. It is time to stand up for the doer, the achiever, the one who sets out to do something and does it; the one who recognizes the problems and opportunities at hand, and deals with them, and is successful, and is not worrying about the failings of others; the one who is constantly looking for more to do; the one who carries the work of the world on his shoulders. The leader. We will never create a good society, much less a great one, until individual excellence is respected and encouraged."

CHAPTER EIGHTEEN

TRUST & CONFIDENCE

I have used the words *trust and confidence* throughout this book to explain just how important it is to establish good lines of communication with the people who live and work in the neighborhoods being served by law enforcement. Absent trust and good communication, any policing strategy is bound to fail.

Trust and confidence are built by following through on the delivery of solid, professionally-based police services. Response times are every bit as important to the caller with a small problem as they are to the caller reporting a major crime in progress. All calls require sincere attention, not a "we'll get to it when we can" mentality.

While at District Three, an alderman contacted me to discuss a problem brought to his attention by a constituent. Earlier, the alderman had contacted a police supervisor downtown, who promised that personnel would be assigned to check into the matter. Several weeks had passed, but nothing had been done to resolve the issue. After obtaining the particulars from the alderman, I passed the details to the sergeant in-charge of the ASP unit. Later that afternoon, a subject was in custody. I then telephoned the alderman and related that the problem had been resolved with an arrest. I further suggested that, should any further problems present themselves, the alderman should simply bring them to my attention.

On another occasion, a neighborhood group leader related to me that she had contacted a district lieutenant about problems with out-of-control teenagers. "You think you have problems," the lieutenant told the woman. "That's nothing compared to what's going on in another part of the District."

I am not suggesting that commanders attend these meetings and simply stroke people to score political points; however, those who take time out their busy lives to attend a meeting and raise concerns should not

63

be marginalized by comparing their complaints to others. Doing so gives the impression that some problems are unworthy of a police response. It is the duty and responsibility of a commanding officer to find resources and then implement a strategy to alleviate problems brought to his or her attention. At a minimum, those in charge should follow-up with residents, gather feedback, and evaluate the police response to the issue. This on-going, persistent sifting of a problem-oriented response strategy will improve the delivery of police services.

As far as overall response times, a police department's dispatch strategy that prioritizes calls for service is fine so long as those who call receive an adequate response. In many instances, individuals contacting the police wish to speak directly to an officer. There are exceptions, of course, such as a caller wishing to report suspicious activity on an anonymous basis. These circumstances merit a squad being dispatched to make their own assessment of the situation or contacting the caller by telephone to gather the details needed to develop a reasonable suspicion for a stop. Should a department's dispatch policy include a directive that officers not be sent unless a caller is observing the suspicious activity, a chilling effect might result; whereby, the perception of the community might soon become one that the police are either inept, lazy, or simply do not care. Those with law enforcement experience know that simply because the caller no longer has sight of the suspicious person doesn't mean a crime is not being committed. Department Policy should be encouraging people to make such calls if the goal of the Police Department is to reduce crime, fear and disorder.

The following are excerpts of some comments I made on a blog regarding a local issue involving a former Pakistani police officer—one who emigrated to the United States—whose attempt to open a business was being stonewalled by a Milwaukee alderman:

> I've been thinking about this ever since I first read the story a couple weeks ago in the Journal. I always had a problem with automatically holding a business accountable for the actions of thugs who decide to make that particular location their C.P. (Command Post). The Nuisance Ordinance was written for that

purpose and was often employed by Commanding Officers in a manner which placed all responsibility on the business owner or building premises owner (in the case of apartment buildings) to take steps to eliminate the problem without taking the initiative to address the crime problems proactively with their own Police resources.

Utilization of the Nuisance Ordinance by Commanding Officers was very strongly encouraged by the Assistant Chief of Police and his Patrol Bureau Deputy Chief both of whom were responding robotically to the complaints of the Commissioner of Neighborhood Services who was complaining that the Ordinance wasn't being used enough. C.O.s were originally supposed to exercise discretion, however it turned into an almost quota-like operation with C.O.s having to explain to the Assistant and Deputy Chiefs why they weren't using the Ordinance more often.

As relates to Judy's and the area near N. 27th and Kilbourn, when I first took command of District Three in November 2001 there was a lot of crime in that area. The crime ranged from minor misdemeanor thefts to drug dealing, armed robberies and shootings. The alderman at that time, Paul Henningsen, was calling my Office and sending information about problems in and around that area and was rightfully demanding something be done about those problems.

My response was to assign foot patrol officers and teams of Area Saturation Patrol (ASP) Officers to address the crime problems with no-nonsense policing which mandated summary arrests for any and all offenses. My Community Liaison Officer and I then began to work with the business owners and apartment building owners to post "No Trespassing/Loitering" signs and to be complainants for any such violations.

Only when/if an owner failed to work with us to help clean up the area did I drop the Nuisance Ordinance bomb on them. It was my philosophy that trust and confidence needed to be built with these people before I could start making demands of them to cooperate with us. If I showed them what we would be doing to clean up the area, then they would have incentive to help us do the job.

During my two years as C.O. of District Three we made significant improvements in that area and many other problem areas of the District because we did what cops are supposed to do – we created an inhospitable environment for the bad guys and gave the good people a sense of security with the knowledge that if they reported problems to us we'd address those problems in a very timely manner. The good people loved us and the bad guys feared us – as it should be.

My point here is that I do not believe that the business necessarily causes the problem (although there have been examples of that with some night clubs), and I would opt to give this new guy the opportunity to do what he says he's going to do given the information that is currently on the table.

And this from another entry on that blog:

Yesterday's hearing at City Hall was very interesting and exhaustive. It began at around 9AM and was still going with closing statements of some Committee members when I left at 3PM. The Committee Chairman, Alderman Jim Bohl, is to be commended for the manner in which he conducted this hearing. It was no nonsense for either side. I did not testify until about 2PM, and I would add that there was no break for lunch either.

Those who were opposed to Mr. Khan included some residents, some business owners, a security person who my Officers worked closely with during my time at #3, and at least one representative of a Neighborhood Group whom I had the pleasure of working with when I was the Commanding Officer of Police District Three. Of course, my testimony was limited to my knowledge of the District during my time there from November 2001 until my reassignment in the middle of December 2003, however I was able to inform the Committee of the need to closely look at the number of calls for service to any specific location and not merely assume that all of those calls for service involved direct problems with the specific location.

For example, someone at a specific location could give the address they were calling from but could be reporting something happening across the street. A burglary during hours which the establishment is closed is also something that cannot necessarily be a problem associated with a poor establishment. That said, I have no reason to dispute anything the opponents reported as relates to crime on or near the premises and certainly have absolutely no reason to defend the previous owners as I believe there was more than enough testimony to substantiate their poor operation of the business.

I would not even make any effort to defend the owner of the building itself. Note that Mr. Khan is not the building owner. He is someone who wants to run a business out of that location and who I am convinced is willing to make the necessary repairs and take the necessary steps to work with the Police Department and residents and other business owners to prevent a reoccurrence of the problems that were there before he arrived on scene.

An argument made by Alderman Bauman and echoed by others who were there to contest Mr. Khan was that the business itself, Judy's, was a detriment to the neighborhood and a magnet for criminal activity and there was no way any new management would change that. During my testimony I used myself as an example of why that was wrong.

I proceeded to tell the Committee and all others that when I was sent by Chief Jones to Command District Three he told me "I need you to do there what you did at District Five". He knew that I had established a policing strategy and crime fighting philosophy which significantly reduced crime in District Five and furthermore attended to the concerns of the people of the various neighborhoods in the District.

He wanted me to do that in District Three. That was a daunting task as District Three had a reputation of being a high crime District almost out of control. For those not familiar with D-3, one of its most notorious neighborhoods was Metcalfe Park aka: the killing fields in 2001.

The area of 27th and Wells-Kilbourn was also plagued with crimes of all types ranging from thefts to shootings and everything in between. For the sake of brevity, we reduced crime in all of these areas and by significant percentages for the two years I was in Command. We did this by giving individual attention to these different areas and working with the good people who lived and worked in these areas and were willing to cooperate with us.

First, we had to establish trust and confidence with them by showing them we were going to do the job they had every right to expect of their Police Department. After explaining to the Committee what we did and how we did it, I said that I was living proof that new management can make a difference and suggested that Mr. Khan could do the same for the Judy's location.

RECOMMENDATIONS

CRIME TREND ANALYSIS

Detectives and officers who have the responsibility of interrogating prisoners should attempt to ascertain why the suspect targeted a particular neighborhood. The answers to these types of questions may prove valuable when commanders allocate resources to prevent and solve future crimes. If weaknesses exist in certain locations, measures can be taken to alter the deployment of officers and/or work schedules can be adjusted. Sometimes, all that is required is working in conjunction with neighborhood groups and business owners to harden potential targets.

CRITIQUE ALL MAJOR INCIDENTS-INCLUDING OFFICERS KILLED/INJURED

A 1957 movie about Marine Corps Recruit Training, titled **The D.I.** and starring Jack Webb as a Marine Corps Drill Instructor, opened with a scene of the D.I.'s office and a plaque that hung over a doorway which read: "Let's be damned sure that no man's ghost will ever say, 'If your training program had only done its job'."

The law enforcement administrator who fails to teach, and who fails to demand that his subordinates teach others, is guilty, in my opinion, of neglect of duty. Experiences—good, bad or indifferent—must be critiqued. The knowledge disseminated from officer debriefings serves as a teachable moment so that success is reinforced and mistakes are not repeated. The belief by some that knowledge is power and, in an effort to protect one's turf or particular assignment, should not be shared has no place in law enforcement. Unlike those Hollywood movies, where detectives work 24 hours a day and never summon back-up, successful policing is predicated upon the concept of team work. This means that subordinates should be willing recipients of the knowledge veterans can offer. A real leader understands that a major part of his/her responsibility is developing future generations of men and women who will someday lead when today's commanders are long retired. Passing knowledge down from one generation to another should be a self-perpetuating process.

Nobody likes to be second guessed. Yet, if something can be learned from a tragedy, the lessons should be studied and critiqued at regular in-service training. It is paramount that young officers learn from the experiences of those who have gone before them. Debriefings were once a regular practice after every tactical situation during my tenure with TEU. No one, no matter their rank or experience, was spared during these critiques.

The FBI has conducted several studies concerning the tactical methods of police officers slain in the line of duty, as well as the characteristics of the suspects (see Appendix for reference material). It would be foolish to ignore the lessons learned from these tragedies.

USE OF OVERTIME GRANT MONEY

When I took command of District Five in 2001, I was informed by Capt. Tony Hendricks, of the MPD's Administration Bureau, that grant money was available to muster resources. In the past, grant money was used to deploy extra patrol units staffed by officers willing to work four or eight hour blocks of overtime. In many instances, officers working these grants patrolled specific hot spots and were generally exempted from responding to routine calls for service. This type of deployment was an honor system of sorts, where officers were expected to generate activity that would deter criminal activity. Any officer could volunteer, which meant management did not have the ability to select officers for these grants. Instead, the administration mandated that a so-called "fair sheet" be kept, virtually guaranteeing that some of the grant officers would emanate from the coat hanger class. A Lieutenant I had worked for in the early 1980s had coined the term "coat hangers" to describe officers who did little more than "hold up the uniform". Typically, the coat hanger would drive around and do the minimal amount of work required to "earn" their overtime pay.

I took a different approach when using this Grant money. I set up the program with the Area Saturation Patrol objective in mind. That meant staffing the basic squads that answered calls for service with two Officers. Since I had already been doing that with our regular Department overtime (without asking permission that I would probably still be waiting for today), I set this Grant overtime project up to staff our basic squads with these overtime volunteers.

They may not have exercised any individual initiative, but they wouldn't just be able to ride around building a resume` to be cab drivers or to deliver flowers when they retired. They were going to actually have to respond to radio calls and would be held accountable if they didn't.

The ASP Officers knew they were going to generate a great deal of activity which would result in their own overtime either at the end of their Shift or in resulting court related overtime. I was able to keep the heat on the thugs with our ASP Officers and play the hand I was dealt from my bosses by using the Grant money and the people I was required to use. It was what some refer to as a Win-Win strategy.

In a government setting, being a leader often mandates that a commander work through or around the rules in order to get the most bang for the taxpayers' buck. In too many instances bureaucrats, content with simply checking the boxes needed to collect their pay, lose sight of the fact that residents living in troubled neighborhoods depend on the police to maintain order.

CONCLUSION

I wrote this book to share what I had learned during my time as a rookie cop through my days as a Commanding Officer of two of Milwaukee's most crime ridden Police Districts. Area Saturation Patrol was a concept that developed over that time as a result of having the great fortune to work around some excellent Police Officers, Detectives and Supervisors who were willing to share their knowledge and experiences with me by word and by example. They laid a foundation upon which I was able to build a policing strategy that worked to combat crime very well and enhance the Quality of Life for many good people in the City of Milwaukee. It was also a policing strategy that allowed good cops to do the job they signed on to do, which was to catch bad guys and put them in jail.

As I write this conclusion, I continue to read about violent crime in the City of Milwaukee and elsewhere across the country, and it bothers me that more emphasis is placed on not "offending" bad guys than on making neighborhoods safer for good people. Some big city Police Chiefs hold press conferences and thump on their chest with statistics that show "crime is down", yet I keep reading about shootings and other violent crime and have to wonder what those people living in these thug infested neighborhoods think. The media only briefly ever takes the time to interview real victims and their families, but when they do I often read about people saying that their neighborhoods are out of control and they are going to move out of their neighborhoods as soon as they can. I don't know how any Police Chief or politician can ignore that and not be personally offended that thugs are taking over parts of their City. The think tank cabals and professional hand wringers can talk all they want to about bad parenting; single parent families; poverty causing crime; not enough YMCAs; not enough federal or state dollars; but the bottom line is that it is the responsibility of the Police Chief to maintain law and order. As for politicians, it really doesn't take a rocket scientist to figure out that if your City is considered safe then it is far more likely businesses will stay and you'll attract more businesses to your City which in turn will increase employment and your tax base.

I have tried to outline a plan that worked and is flexible enough to adapt in big or small cities if the will is there among administrators and residents to address crime problems in their jurisdictions. It requires teamwork and a willingness to spend money to properly staff and equip their police departments as well as to build jails and prisons to house those responsible for crime and the reduction of Quality of Life for good people. Too often I hear about how much it costs to house prisoners. My immediate response is "How much does it cost to allow them to roam free and terrorize decent folk? What's an innocent life worth to you?"

Area Saturation Patrol, as I have outlined it in this book, is admittedly an extreme strategy to combat crime, but years of "diversion" programs; "alternative sentencing"; probation; and light prison sentences with early parole to "relieve prison overcrowding", has done nothing to stop these same thugs from terrorizing neighborhoods. They have become more emboldened too and don't seem to be afraid of cops anymore. When the thugs run as a pack, the only way to deal with them is for a special unit of Police Officers to run as a pack. Failure to recognize that will result in out of control neighborhoods and eventually out of control cities.

CAPTAIN GLENN D. FRANKOVIS

ABOUT THE AUTHOR:

Glenn D. Frankovis, is a retired Milwaukee Police Department (MPD) captain (1975-2004), who served as commanding officer of Districts Five and Three. Over the course of his career, he was assigned to the MPD's Tactical Enforcement Unit, both as a police officer and as a sergeant. Frankovis was also a district-level street supervisor and, as a lieutenant, a district shift commander.

Thank you to Lynn Hubbard for her formatting design.

Special thanks to Andy Smith who helped layout this book that is dedicated to those law enforcement officers who understand that the function of a lawman is to stand between the good people and thugs.

SERVICE AWARDS:

- June 19, 2002 - Law Enforcement Coordination Honor Award presented to me at the National Weed & Seed Conference in New Orleans, Louisiana by the Executive Director of the Weed & Seed Program (U.S. Attorney's Office) for the 2001 Street Sweeper Operation initiated while I was the Commanding Officer of the Fifth District. (This award was one of only five awards presented nationally for innovative concepts related to crime reduction and followed a similar award presented to me by the Milwaukee Exchange Club upon nomination by the U.S. Attorney's Office-Weed and Seed Program in Milwaukee.)
- July 17, 2002 - Milwaukee Common Council Proclamation Award recognizing the above national award presented to me and recognizing my service to the Milwaukee Police Department and citizens of Milwaukee.
- April 01, 2003 - Certificate presented to me from the principal of Phillis Wheatley Elementary School "in honor and recognition of (my) outstanding 'Service to the Community'.
- June 13, 2003 - Award from the principal of Washington High School, Dr. Connor, which stated: "For outstanding leadership and supporting a safe learning environment at Washington High School".
- January 20, 2004 - Community Service Award from Marquette University Public Safety Department
- February 03, 2004 - Recognition by the Washington Heights Neighborhood Association at their annual meeting for service to the residents and business owners during my tenure as the District #3 Commanding Officer.

- In May 2001, I directed P.O. Juanita Carr (District #5's Auxiliary Police Officer coordinator) to supplement the two bicycle officers who are assigned to patrol the east side bicycle path and Lakefront during the summer months. Her duties included foot patrol of the upper bicycle path with auxiliary officers, which would then permit the two bicycle officers to patrol the southern end of the bike path and the Lakefront itself. In past years it was not unusual to have robberies and an occasional sexual assault reported along the bike path during the summer months. In 2001, during the summer months, no major crimes were reported on the east side bike path. I expanded this use of Auxiliary Officers to include periodic foot patrol of a variety of areas in District #5 which were in need of such patrol and which addressed concerns raised to me during my meetings with various neighborhood groups.

- Upon my arrival at District #5 in February, I was informed that $43,500 of overtime Weed & Seed Grant money was available to me for use in fighting crime. From past experience, I knew that our Area Saturation Patrol officers were not able to man ASP squads regularly during the summer months due to manpower shortages resulting from summer vacations and other summertime special events requiring District personnel. I also suspected that the Global Pension Settlement would result in an additional drain on our manpower due to increased retirements. I decided to use the money to staff Early and Late Shift squad cars officers working 4 hour blocks of overtime using the Weed & Seed grant money. I commenced the Directed Patrol Mission (DPM) using the Weed & Seed Grant Money at the end of May during Memorial Day weekend. The overtime money lasted through the first week of September and allowed us to field two person basic squad cars on the Early Shift and full complements of ASP squads, which in turn permitted us to conduct the very successful Street Sweeper operations.

APPENDIX

Milwaukee Police Department

January 1 through December 31

District One Reported Part I Offenses

	2002	2001	Diff	% Change
Aggravated Assault	75	71	4	5.6%
Arson	1	6	-5	-83.3%
Burglary	96	70	26	37.1%
Homicide	1	3	-2	-66.7%
Motor Vehicle Theft	177	234	-57	-24.4%
Robbery	47	57	-10	-17.5%
Forcible Sex Offenses	12	20	-8	-40.0%
Theft Offenses	1574	1658	-84	-5.1%
Total Part I Offenses	1983	2119	-136	-6.4%
Shootings	1	5	-4	-80.0%

District Five Reported Part I Offenses

	2002	2001	Diff	% Change
Aggravated Assault	783	831	-48	-5.8%
Arson	66	91	-25	-27.5%
Burglary	1126	1130	-4	-0.4%
Homicide	36	20	16	80.0%
Motor Vehicle Theft	1254	1321	-67	-5.1%
Robbery	592	603	-11	-1.8%
Forcible Sex Offenses	142	188	-46	-24.5%
Theft Offenses	5584	5061	523	10.3%
Total Part I Offenses	9583	9245	338	3.7%
Shootings	132	129	3	2.3%

District Two Reported Part I Offenses

	2002	2001	Diff	% Change
Aggravated Assault	540	461	79	17.1%
Arson	75	105	-30	-28.6%
Burglary	1052	981	71	7.2%
Homicide	12	16	-4	-25.0%
Motor Vehicle Theft	883	959	-76	-7.9%
Robbery	363	365	-2	-0.5%
Forcible Sex Offenses	109	144	-35	-24.3%
Theft Offenses	3222	3410	-188	-5.5%
Total Part I Offenses	6256	6441	-185	-2.9%
Shootings	86	64	22	34.4%

District Six Reported Part I Offenses

	2002	2001	Diff	% Change
Aggravated Assault	427	392	35	8.9%
Arson	49	50	-1	-2.0%
Burglary	680	754	-74	-9.8%
Homicide	3	12	-9	-75.0%
Motor Vehicle Theft	707	698	9	1.3%
Robbery	262	264	-2	-0.8%
Forcible Sex Offenses	81	130	-49	-37.7%
Theft Offenses	2670	2828	-158	-5.6%
Total Part I Offenses	4879	5128	-249	-4.9%
Shootings	59	32	27	84.4%

District Three Reported Part I Offenses

	2002	2001	Diff	% Change
Aggravated Assault	811	992	-181	-18.2%
Arson	72	74	-2	-2.7%
Burglary	962	1166	-204	-17.5%
Homicide	18	35	-17	-48.6%
Motor Vehicle Theft	1279	1254	25	2.0%
Robbery	625	632	-7	-1.1%
Forcible Sex Offenses	160	199	-39	-19.6%
Theft Offenses	3868	4126	-258	-6.3%
Total Part I Offenses	7795	8478	-683	-8.1%
Shootings	107	187	-80	-42.8%

District Seven Reported Part I Offenses

	2002	2001	Diff	% Change
Aggravated Assault	1078	1010	68	6.7%
Arson	111	122	-11	-9.0%
Burglary	1974	1799	175	9.7%
Homicide	28	33	-5	-15.2%
Motor Vehicle Theft	1837	2175	-338	-15.5%
Robbery	882	762	120	15.7%
Forcible Sex Offenses	201	262	-61	-23.3%
Theft Offenses	5493	5265	228	4.3%
Total Part I Offenses	11604	11428	176	1.5%
Shootings	171	154	17	11.0%

District Four Reported Part I Offenses

	2002	2001	Diff	% Change
Aggravated Assault	502	526	-24	-4.6%
Arson	35	45	-10	-22.2%
Burglary	773	874	-101	-11.6%
Homicide	10	8	2	25.0%
Motor Vehicle Theft	1004	1249	-245	-19.6%
Robbery	410	342	68	19.9%
Forcible Sex Offenses	141	152	-11	-7.2%
Theft Offenses	3618	3382	236	7.0%
Total Part I Offenses	6493	6578	-85	-1.3%
Shootings	45	49	-4	-8.2%

City Wide Reported Part I Offenses

	2002	2001	Diff	% Change
Aggravated Assault	4216	4283	-67	-1.6%
Arson	409	493	-84	-17.0%
Burglary	6663	6774	-111	-1.6%
Homicide	108	127	-19	-15.0%
Motor Vehicle Theft	7141	7890	-749	-9.5%
Robbery	3181	3025	156	5.2%
Forcible Sex Offenses	846	1095	-249	-22.7%
Theft Offenses	26029	25730	299	1.2%
Total Part I Offenses	48593	49417	-824	-1.7%
Shootings	601	620	-19	-3.1%

*Data not edited for Uniform Crime Reporting.

887 Reports in Tickler File as of 1/6/03

Crime Analysis Section
6-Jan-03

District One Reported Part I Offenses

	2003	2002	Diff	% Change
Aggravated Assault	65	78	-13	-16.7%
Arson	0	1	-1	-100.0%
Burglary	135	101	34	33.7%
Homicide	0	1	-1	-100.0%
Motor Vehicle Theft	157	177	-20	-11.3%
Robbery	49	48	1	2.1%
Forcible Sex Offenses	12	12	0	0.0%
Theft Offenses	1594	1605	-11	-0.7%
Total Part I Offenses	*2012*	*2023*	*-11*	-0.5%
Shootings	3	1	2	200.0%

District Two Reported Part I Offenses

	2003	2002	Diff	% Change
Aggravated Assault	532	549	-17	-3.1%
Arson	60	76	-16	-21.1%
Burglary	805	1067	-262	-24.6%
Homicide	12	12	0	0.0%
Motor Vehicle Theft	755	886	-131	-14.8%
Robbery	377	365	12	3.3%
Forcible Sex Offenses	86	119	-33	-27.7%
Theft Offenses	3226	3268	-42	-1.3%
Total Part I Offenses	*5853*	*6342*	*-489*	-7.7%
Shootings	83	89	-6	-6.7%

District Three Reported Part I Offenses

	2003	2002	Diff	% Change
Aggravated Assault	701	819	-118	-14.4%
Arson	73	73	0	0.0%
Burglary	868	976	-108	-11.1%
Homicide	30	17	13	76.5%
Motor Vehicle Theft	1228	1281	-53	-4.1%
Robbery	491	627	-136	-21.7%
Forcible Sex Offenses	153	165	-12	-7.3%
Theft Offenses	3837	3934	-97	-2.5%
Total Part I Offenses	*7381*	*7892*	*-511*	-6.5%
Shootings	112	108	4	3.7%

District Four Reported Part I Offenses

	2003	2002	Diff	% Change
Aggravated Assault	442	506	-64	-12.6%
Arson	39	35	4	11.4%
Burglary	891	784	107	13.6%
Homicide	10	10	0	0.0%
Motor Vehicle Theft	928	1007	-79	-7.8%
Robbery	342	413	-71	-17.2%
Forcible Sex Offenses	134	153	-19	-12.4%
Theft Offenses	3294	3685	-391	-10.6%
Total Part I Offenses	*6080*	*6593*	*-513*	-7.8%
Shootings	45	47	-2	-4.3%

District Five Reported Part I Offenses

	2003	2002	Diff	% Change
Aggravated Assault	686	794	-108	-13.6%
Arson	58	67	-9	-13.4%
Burglary	920	1145	-225	-19.7%
Homicide	20	37	-17	-45.9%
Motor Vehicle Theft	1055	1256	-201	-16.0%
Robbery	541	598	-57	-9.5%
Forcible Sex Offenses	110	149	-39	-26.2%
Theft Offenses	5257	5652	-395	-7.0%
Total Part I Offenses	*8647*	*9698*	*-1051*	-10.8%
Shootings	106	133	-27	-20.3%

District Six Reported Part I Offenses

	2003	2002	Diff	% Change
Aggravated Assault	379	431	-52	-12.1%
Arson	39	49	-10	-20.4%
Burglary	611	687	-76	-11.1%
Homicide	8	3	5	166.7%
Motor Vehicle Theft	616	711	-95	-13.4%
Robbery	266	263	3	1.1%
Forcible Sex Offenses	74	93	-19	-20.4%
Theft Offenses	2671	2713	-42	-1.5%
Total Part I Offenses	*4664*	*4950*	*-286*	-5.8%
Shootings	43	60	-17	-28.3%

District Seven Reported Part I Offenses

	2003	2002	Diff	% Change
Aggravated Assault	1060	1085	-25	-2.3%
Arson	89	114	-25	-21.9%
Burglary	1797	2001	-204	-10.2%
Homicide	26	28	-2	-7.1%
Motor Vehicle Theft	1498	1845	-347	-18.8%
Robbery	879	884	-5	-0.6%
Forcible Sex Offenses	183	209	-26	-12.4%
Theft Offenses	5485	5612	-127	-2.3%
Total Part I Offenses	*11017*	*11778*	*-761*	-6.5%
Shootings	186	173	13	7.5%

City Wide Reported Part I Offenses

	2003	2002	Diff	% Change
Aggravated Assault	3865	4262	-397	-9.3%
Arson	358	415	-57	-13.7%
Burglary	6027	6761	-734	-10.9%
Homicide	106	108	-2	-1.9%
Motor Vehicle Theft	6237	7163	-926	-12.9%
Robbery	2945	3198	-253	-7.9%
Forcible Sex Offenses	752	900	-148	-16.4%
Theft Offenses	25364	26469	-1105	-4.2%
Total Part I Offenses	*45654*	*49276*	*-3622*	-7.4%
Shootings	578	611	-33	-5.4%

*Data not edited for Uniform Crime Reporting.

NC = Not Calculable

328 Reports in Tickler File as of 1/6/04

Crime Analysis Section
6-Jan-04

Reported Violent Crime
January 1 through December 31

District One Reported Violent Crime

	2003	2002	Diff	% Change
Aggravated Assault	65	78	-13	-16.7%
Forcible Sex Offenses	12	12	0	0.0%
Homicide	0	1	-1	-100.0%
Robbery	49	48	1	2.1%
Total Violent Crime	126	139	-13	-9.4%

District Two Reported Violent Crime

	2003	2002	Diff	% Change
Aggravated Assault	532	549	-17	-3.1%
Forcible Sex Offenses	86	119	-33	-27.7%
Homicide	12	12	0	0.0%
Robbery	377	365	12	3.3%
Total Violent Crime	1007	1045	-38	-3.6%

District Three Reported Violent Crime

	2003	2002	Diff	% Change
Aggravated Assault	701	819	-118	-14.4%
Forcible Sex Offenses	153	165	-12	-7.3%
Homicide	30	17	13	76.5%
Robbery	491	627	-136	-21.7%
Total Violent Crime	1375	1628	-253	-15.5%

District Four Reported Violent Crime

	2003	2002	Diff	% Change
Aggravated Assault	442	506	-64	-12.6%
Forcible Sex Offenses	134	153	-19	-12.4%
Homicide	10	10	0	0.0%
Robbery	342	413	-71	-17.2%
Total Violent Crime	928	1082	-154	-14.2%

District Five Reported Violent Crime

	2003	2002	Diff	% Change
Aggravated Assault	686	794	-108	-13.6%
Forcible Sex Offenses	110	149	-39	-26.2%
Homicide	20	37	-17	-45.9%
Robbery	541	598	-57	-9.5%
Total Violent Crime	1357	1578	-221	-14.0%

District Six Reported Violent Crime

	2003	2002	Diff	% Change
Aggravated Assault	379	431	-52	-12.1%
Forcible Sex Offenses	74	93	-19	-20.4%
Homicide	8	3	5	166.7%
Robbery	266	263	3	1.1%
Total Violent Crime	727	790	-63	-8.0%

District Seven Reported Violent Crime

	2003	2002	Diff	% Change
Aggravated Assault	1060	1085	-25	-2.3%
Forcible Sex Offenses	183	209	-26	-12.4%
Homicide	26	28	-2	-7.1%
Robbery	879	884	-5	-0.6%
Total Violent Crime	2148	2206	-58	-2.6%

City Wide Reported Violent Crime

	2003	2002	Diff	% Change
Aggravated Assault	3865	4262	-397	-9.3%
Forcible Sex Offenses	752	900	-148	-16.4%
Homicide	106	108	-2	-1.9%
Robbery	2945	3198	-253	-7.9%
Total Violent Crime	7668	8468	-800	-9.4%

*Data not edited for Uniform Crime Reporting.
NC = Not Calculable
328 Reports in Tickler File as of 1/6/04

Crime Analysis Section
6-Jan-04

SUMMARY ARREST FOR MUNICIPAL ORDINANCE VIOLATIONS

Upheld by the United States Supreme Court
SUPREME COURT OF THE UNITED STATES

[10]   ATWATER et al. v. CITY OF LAGO VISTA et al.

[11]   Certiorari To The United States Court Of Appeals For The Fifth Circuit

[12]   No. 99-1408.

[13]   Argued December 4, 2000

[14]   Decided April 24, 2001

"Texas law makes it a misdemeanor, punishable only by a fine, either for a front-seat passenger in a car equipped with safety belts not to wear one or for the driver to fail to secure any small child riding in front. The warrantless arrest of anyone violating these provisions is expressly authorized by statute, but the police may issue citations in lieu of arrest. Petitioner Atwater drove her truck in Lago Vista, Texas, with her small children in the front seat. None of them was wearing a seatbelt. Respondent Turek, then a Lago Vista policeman, observed the seatbelt violations, pulled Atwater over, verbally berated her, handcuffed her, placed her in his squad car, and drove her to the local police station, where she was made to remove her shoes, jewelry, and eyeglasses, and empty her pockets. Officers took her "mug shot" and placed her, alone, in a jail cell for about an hour, after which she was taken before a magistrate and released on bond. She was charged with, among other things, violating the seatbelt law. She pleaded no contest to the seatbelt misdemeanors and paid a $50 fine. She and her husband (collectively Atwater) filed suit under 42 U. S. C. §1983, alleging, inter alia, that the actions of respondents (collectively City) had violated her Fourth Amendment right to be free from unreasonable seizure. Given her admission that she had violated the law and the absence of any allegation that she was harmed or detained in any way inconsistent with the law, the District Court ruled the Fourth Amendment claim meritless and granted the City summary judgment. Sitting en banc, the Fifth Circuit affirmed. Relying on Wren v. United States, 517 U. S. 806, 817-818, the court observed that, although the Fourth Amendment generally requires a balancing of individual and governmental interests, the result is rarely in doubt where an arrest is based on probable cause. Because no one disputed that Turek had probable cause to arrest Atwater, and there was no evidence the arrest was conducted in an extraordinary manner, unusually harmful to Atwater's privacy interests, the court held the arrest not unreasonable for Fourth Amendment purposes.

[16]   Held: The Fourth Amendment does not forbid a warrantless arrest for a minor criminal offense, such as a misdemeanor seatbelt violation punishable only by a fine. Pp. 4-33."

RECEIVED

03 MAY -1 PM 2:23

MILWAUKEE POLICE
PATROL BUREAU **MILWAUKEE POLICE DEPARTMENT**

<u>District #3</u>
Thurs., 05-01-2003

REPORT

In the matter of: Summary Arrests & Officer Discretion

To: <u>Dale T. Schunk</u>

<u>Deputy Chief of Police</u>

Sir:

This report is prepared by Captain Glenn D. Frankovis of District #3.

Attached are several Roll Call notes I have written regarding Municipal Ordinance violations and the summary arrest.

At various Roll Calls I have conducted since becoming a supervisor in April of 1981, I have stressed enforcement of all City Ordinances and State Statutes. I am a proponent of the summary arrest as a means of resolving problems, although I do not mandate that every violation must result in a summary arrest. In fact, I have had to issue Roll Call instructions to the contrary (see attached, dated 04-25-2003 Item #1).

Throughout my supervisory career, I have been surprised to learn that some police officers have been under the mistaken impression that they could not make summary arrests for Ordinance violations. In some cases, I have come to the conclusion that some officers prefer not to make summary arrests for their own convenience even though the summary arrest would be absolutely necessary to resolve the situation. In other cases, I have discovered that some supervisors discouraged officers from making the summary arrest. I do not tolerate laziness on the part of officers or supervisors and take immediate corrective action when these things become apparent to me. That corrective action includes meetings with supervisors, Roll Call notes, personal instructions by me at Roll Calls, and on street observations by me to ensure that my instructions are understood.

During my Roll Call presentations, when the subject of Ordinance enforcement and summary arrests comes up, I have explained why the summary arrest is a very important option. I have also taken time to explain that officers still have the authority to exercise discretion, however when I am led to believe that officers are choosing not to arrest violators I look into the reasons. Therefore, I have instructed officers to be prepared to explain to their Lieutenants why they chose the non-

summary over summary course of action. This is the only way I
know to make sure that officers understand their options as set
forth in Department S.O.P. It also allows for education of the
officers by their Lieutenants to broaden their perspective and to
enhance their performance and overall operational efficiency.

Any officer who believes that my philosophy on the summary
arrest applies in all cases, or is designed to adversely impact
on a particular race of people, is exhibiting his/her own
personal bias which is not based on any supportable evidence. It
is also an allegation not shared by anyone who has ever attended
a neighborhood meeting that I was at nor is it an allegation
which has ever been brought to my attention by anyone who has
worked for me. I have solicited input from officers and
supervisors at Roll Calls on many occasions regarding our
operations and suggestions to improve or change our operations.
Anyone having any concerns has had ample opportunity to express
those concerns.

I am proud to say that my no nonsense approach to crime
fighting, and strict enforcement of the laws and ordinances, has
resulted in crime reduction wherever I have worked and is
strongly supported by neighborhood associations and public
officials. My approach has definitely resulted in an increase in
the quality or life for decent people and a significant decrease
in the comfort levels of thugs.

Respectfully submitted,

Captain Glenn D. Frankovis
District #3

To BE READ AT ALL ROLL CALLS UNTIL 1-28-2002 CAPT GDF 1-15

MILWAUKEE POLICE DEPARTMENT
District #3 Memorandum

01/15/2002

TO: ALL SHIFTS - DISTRICT #3

FROM: CAPT. GLENN D. FRANKOVIS *GDF*

RE: ROLL CALL

1) Search your cars thoroughly when taking possession of them after Roll Call; search them thoroughly as soon as possible after you remove someone from the back seat of your squad whether or not that person was under arrest (**never put someone in the back seat of your squad for the sole purpose of conducting an FI - regardless of the weather, unless you sit in the back seat with that person - police officers have been killed because of this mistake**).

2) I will not authorize any <u>voluntary</u> overtime for a member while that member is on FMLA status. The member must honor any subpoenas, and overtime will be authorized for that purpose.

3) You will all be receiving your copies of S.O.P. 3/070.00, dated 1-14-2002, which deals with the guidelines for Arrest/Citation Procedures. Take the time to read and understand it. I want to highlight that part of the S.O.P. which provides guidelines for the enforcement of City Ordinances and the issuance of citations. **"Citation issuance, in lieu of summary arrest, is contingent on whether or not it resolves the situation conclusively. Further, issuance of a citation at the scene of an incident must include verification of either residency or employment within Milwaukee County or a reasonable belief that the violator will appear in Municipal Court on the court date or will stipulate to the citation."**

    3/075.10 (A) 2. **"<u>Not Released</u>: The member shall insert the date and time of the next regular session of the Municipal Court…"**

    3/075.15 (A): **"Suspects shall be released taking into account the following factors:**
      1. **The accused has been properly identified.**
      2. **The accused is willing to sign for receipt of the citation.**
      3. **The accused appears not to represent a danger of harm to himself/herself, another person, or property.**
      4. **The accused can show sufficient evidence of ties to the community.**
      5. **The accused has not previously failed to appear or respond to a citation.**
      6. **Further detention to carry out legitimate investigative action in accordance with Department policies does not appear necessary."**

83

The summary arrest for Municipal Ordinance violations is okay providing that the criteria as set forth above is followed. Therefore, it is absolutely imperative that you articulate your reasons for making the summary arrest, with next regularly scheduled court date, in your narrative. This additional information will dispel any concern as to why a summary arrest was made as opposed to non-summary.

4) Do not put your feet on the walls. It leaves marks which then need to be washed off with soap and water. So unless you are looking for something extra to do, pay heed to this.

5) Your crime fighting efforts have been outstanding. I review all of the copies of PA-45s which are left in the Lieutenant's office. Excellent arrests are being made resulting in a reduction in crime in the Third District and praise from the only people who really matter - the decent folks we are here to protect.

COPY

MILWAUKEE POLICE DEPARTMENT
District #3 Memorandum

10/14/2002

TO: Early/Late Power/Late Shifts - DISTRICT #3

FROM: CAPT. GLENN D. FRANKOVIS

RE: Curfew Enforcement

Every Officer assigned to street duties on the Early/Late Power/Late Shifts shall actively attempt to enforce the Curfew Ordinance on a nightly basis. <u>Unless directed by your Shift Commander to do otherwise, every Curfew citation shall require a Parents' Responsibility citation to also be issued.</u>

MILWAUKEE POLICE DEPARTMENT
District #3 Memorandum

10/16/2002

TO: ALL SHIFTS - DISTRICT #3

FROM: CAPT. GLENN D. FRANKOVIS

RE: ROLL CALL

1)   S.O.P. 2/900.15 deals with Uniform Standards. Section A
     explains the requirements for your nameplates; Section C (2)
     states that you may wear <u>one</u> tie bar or tie tack. <u>If you
     earned a Ceasefire pin, it is to be worn just below the name
     tag at the top of the shirt pocket. If you earned any other
     ribbon authorized by the Chief, it is to be worn below the
     name tag above the pocket and, if you have also earned the
     Ceasefire pin, above that pin.</u> **DO NOT WEAR ANY OTHER PINS
     OR RIBBONS ON YOUR UNIFORM WITHOUT THE APPROVAL OF THE
     CAPTAIN.**

2)   It is everyone's responsibility to enforce the Curfew
     Ordinance and Truancy. I expect this to be accomplished on
     a daily basis by Night shift and Day shift officers and
     their supervisors. The only time you will not issue a
     citation to the parent of a Curfew violator will be when
     authorized not to by your Shift Commander. There will be no
     discretion on this issue except that exercised by your Shift
     Commander.

COPY

MILWAUKEE POLICE DEPARTMENT
District #3 Memorandum

04/14/2003

TO: ALL SHIFTS - DISTRICT #3

FROM: CAPT. GLENN D. FRANKOVIS

RE: ROLL CALL

1) I worked the street Friday night, April 11th until approximately 1:30A.M., and was very favorably impressed with what I saw. Early Shift Officers were looking for an Entry to Auto suspect in the area of 27th and Kilbourn and had put out a good description. Sqd 635A (P.O. Ala Awadallah) was returning to District #3 from the PAB and observed the suspect at 27th and State. The arrest was made and property was recovered. This is what I constantly refer to as the Team Effort. Early, Late Power and Late Shifts did an outstanding job of addressing issues related to the Caribbean Culture Club and Club Platinum as well as keeping our backlog of assignments at an acceptable level.

2) While on the street, I conducted a couple of tavern checks. One of the locations I stopped at was under the impression that they could leave their doors open until 10PM. That's true under City Ordinance 90-27 (2) (attached), **however City Ordinance 80.65(4) b-2 and b-3 prohibit noise at a distance greater than 50 feet to be played in such a manner so as to disturb the peace, quiet and comfort of neighboring occupants. During the course of your patrol, if you should come across a tavern with the doors open and playing music loud enough to be heard from 50 feet away, they are in violation of the Noise Nuisance Ordinance 80.65(4) and can be issued citations for same regardless of the time of day or night.** If you choose to warn them the first time, that's okay with me. Warnings require follow up to ensure compliance. Subsequent violations are to be dealt with by issuing citations and writing Tavern Reports. If you had previously warned the tavern manager or bartender, include that information in your report and on your citation specifying who it was that you had previously warned and when.

MILWAUKEE POLICE DEPARTMENT
District #3 Memorandum

04/25/2003

TO: ALL SHIFTS - DISTRICT #3

FROM: CAPT. GLENN D. FRANKOVIS *GDF*

RE: ROLL CALL

1) Routine traffic stops for violations which would ordinarily be non summary court dates to Municipal Court are not to result in summary arrests unless approved by your Shift Commander. The exceptions would be if you had probable cause to make a summary arrest for an Ordinance or State Statute violation (D.C; Obstructing; etc.) or if the person driving does not have a driver's license and there is no other way to verify the identity of the driver. In the case of OAWOOL, that would be the basis for the summary arrest. The traffic violation, in and of itself, will not ordinarily be cause for a summary arrest.

2) On May 3rd, 2003, from 9AM to 4:30PM, the Special Olympics will be holding their annual track and field events at Nicolet High School in Glendale. If you are interested in assisting with the presentation of medals, you are authorized to wear your uniform. Call 1-262-241-7786 for further information.

3) S.O.P. 3/080.00 (A - F) Transportation of Arrestees is attached and to be read at all Roll Calls.

4) State Statute 346.03(5) requires you to operate your squad cars with due regard for the safety of others. Remember, just because you have your red lights and siren on does not relieve you of the responsibility to proceed safely. You still must slow down and/or stop before proceeding through red lights or stop signs.

5) Keep the clip board in your squad secured and off the dash board to prevent it from interfering with the safe operation of your vehicle.

6) Exercise extreme care when executing any type of U-turn – even when operating as an emergency vehicle.

7) Replacement officers are to submit green (paid) overtime cards only, and the code is always 1635.

8) If your comp balance is 225 or more hours (128 for supervisors), you are not to take anymore comp overtime unless you are in the band. Check with your Shift Commander or Desk Sergeant if you need to.

9) When you inventory items which contain other items (purse; suitcase; etc.), you must check for valuables and inventory them separately on the same inventory with the container you took them out of.

MILWAUKEE POLICE DEPARTMENT
District #3 Memorandum

04/25/2003

TO: ALL SHIFTS - DISTRICT #3

FROM: CAPT. GLENN D. FRANKOVIS

RE: ROLL CALL

1) 4211 W. Spaulding is not getting along with 4215/17 W. Spaulding. If you get sent to any problems at those locations, and there is probable cause to issue a citation and/or make an arrest -**DO IT!**

2) I have received complaints about loud music and other nuisance conduct coming from and around 4252 W. Highland. I want strict enforcement to encourage people to conform to the neighborhood norms. If you hear the loud music, you do not need an outside complainant to issue citations. Your callers for this one may elect to remain anonymous. Don't allow that fact to keep you from taking action.

authorized by state statute 343.16, shall date and sign the report and forward it to the Accident Investigator's Section.

3/075.00 MUNICIPAL COURT CITATIONS

Milwaukee Uniform Municipal Court Citations (Form CBP-200) and Milwaukee Municipal Court Juvenile Citations (Form CBP-201) shall be used for city ordinance violations denoted on the current Municipal Court Deposit Schedule.

A. GENERAL GUIDELINES

Citation issuance, in lieu of summary arrest, is contingent on whether or not it resolves the situation conclusively. Further, issuance of a citation at the scene of an incident must include verification of either residency or
employment within Milwaukee County or a reasonable belief that the violator will appear in Municipal Court on the court date or will stipulate to the citation. The court date is listed in the monthly "Municipal Court Schedule."

B. SPECIAL CATEGORIES

1. Retail Theft

Any individual apprehended for retail theft is to be summarily arrested if one of the following criteria is met:

a. The retail (actual sticker price) before taxes is $100 or more.
b. Suspect has a prior felony, no matter how old.
c. Suspect has a prior theft or theft-related conviction.
d. Suspect is on probation or parole.
e. Suspect was using special or professional shoplifting devices.

2. Boating Violations

Form CBP-200 and Form CBP-201 can only be used for boating violations covered by city ordinance which are noncriminal. The Wisconsin Uniform Boating Citation (Form 4100-70) must be used for criminal boating violations as well as for boating violations not covered by city ordinance. These violations are only returnable to Circuit Court. The Special Operations Bureau Commander shall establish a procedure for processing and filing the Wisconsin Uniform Boating Citations.

3. Bicycle Violations

In cases of violations of Section 102-2 of the Ordinances (Bicycle License/Registration) violators shall be advised to register the bicycle within five (5) working days after the issuance of the citation and then present proof of compliance at the scheduled court date.

3/075.05 ISSUANCE OF MUNICIPAL CITATION

A. Form CBP-200 and Form CBP-201 are both four-part, serial numbered forms which are to be completed as follows: Department members shall accurately and legibly complete the face of the citation and shall insert the proper ordinance number and total deposit amount as listed in the Municipal Court Deposit Schedule. The proper court date and time must be inserted, as indicated on the Municipal Court Schedule, if no summary arrest is made.

B. Members shall complete the "Proof of Service" section on the reverse side of the green (adult) or blue (juvenile) court copy and they shall have the offender sign same, indicating the offender has received a copy of the citation. If the offender refuses to sign, the word "REFUSED" shall be inserted in the signature block.

C. Adult offenders shall be presented with the white (adult) hard copy, the white City Attorney's copy, and a copy of the citation disposition instructions. Present the juvenile offender with the buff (juvenile) hard copy and the citation disposition instructions copy.

D. Complete the "Incident Report" block on the reverse side of the agency (police) pink copy or canary copy, if juvenile, and sign name. In addition:

1. List all pertinent facts relating to the violation.
2. If a juvenile, insert the name of the parent or guardian and the time notified. Also insert the time that the member released the juvenile.
3. Print the names and addresses of the complainant and witnesses on the bottom line. (This must be completed or the city attorney will not issue charges.)
4. Insert inventory number(s) if such form(s) has been completed.
5. Print off group and your duty hours. Also, list any scheduled vacation or military leave time.

E. The original and remaining copies of Form CBP-200 or Form CBP-201 are to be turned in to the shift commander no later than the end of the tour of duty during which the citation was issued.

3/075.10 CITATIONS FOR SUMMARY ARRESTS OF ADULTS

A. SUMMARY ARRESTS

1. Released

Persons summarily arrested for a city ordinance violation shall, generally, be conveyed to the district station of the district in which the arrest occurred when on-street situations mandate a secure locale. When issuance, identification, and booking are accomplished, such persons shall be released for a future court date.

2. Not Released

In general, the only persons summarily arrested and **not** released for municipal offenses are: "Cash Bail Only" Municipal Writs, city commitments, and city O.W.I. In these cases an Arrest/Detention Report (PA-45) is required. See SOP 3/150.60 The arresting member shall prepare and issue the citation at the time of booking the violator at a district station or the Prisoner Processing Section (PPS). The member shall insert the date and time of the next regular session of the Municipal Court as listed on the "Municipal Court Schedule." Further, if the court is in session, a court liaison officer shall process the violator.

B. LIAISON OFFICER

The Court Administration Section (CAS) "liaison officer" will retain both the Arrest/Detention Report and citations for those summarily arrested and will present the citations to the reviewing assistant city attorney. The assistant city attorney will review and sign both copies of the citation indicating approval for prosecuting or refusal and reason therefor. After processing at the city attorney's office, the liaison officer will forward the reviewed and signed green original and pink copy to Municipal Court.

NOTE: After the initial court hearing, the green and pink copy will be retained in the Municipal\ Court case jacket.

3/075.15 FUTURE COURT DATE RELEASE FOR ADULT MUNICIPAL CITATION ARRESTS

A. Shift commanders shall authorize the release of suspects summarily arrested for violations of municipal ordinances by giving the violator a future court date. The future court date shall be so indicated on the municipal citation and shall be in accordance with the schedule as provided by the "Municipal Court Schedule". Personal Recognizance Bonds are no longer needed to release a suspect summarily arrested on a municipal ordinance violation. Suspects shall be released taking into account the following factors:

1. The accused has been properly identified.
2. The accused is willing to sign for receipt of the citation.
3. The accused appears not to represent a danger of harm to himself/herself, another person, or property.
4. The accused can show sufficient evidence of ties to the community.
5. The accused has not previously failed to appear or respond to a citation.
6. Further detention to carry out legitimate investigative action in accordance with Department policies does not appear necessary.

3/075.20 CITATIONS ISSUED TO ADULTS - NON-SUMMARY

A. Each District/Bureau shall prepare an original and two copies of the transmittal listing sheets Form MC-681 "Listing of Issued Non-Traffic Citations" for each scheduled court date. Citations shall be listed in alphabetical order by violator's last name first. The original transmittal and two copies, together with the original (green) and (pink) citation copy, is to be delivered by police courier to the Court Administration Section on Monday through Friday, except designated city holidays. CAS personnel shall check citations against transmittal listing to ensure all are received. One copy of the transmittal listing sheet shall be retained at the originating district/bureau. Citations shall be forwarded to the CAS within five days of issuance.

B. The liaison officer will present the scheduled citations to the City Attorney's Office for review. After review at the City Attorney's Office, the liaison officer will forward the reviewed and signed green original citation and the pink copy of the citation to Municipal Court. After the court hearing, the green and pink copies shall be filed in the court jacket in the Municipal Court Clerk's Office.

AREA SATURATION PATROL

· BLOCK ASSOCIATION ·

District Two - Powe
P.O. Keith BOCHER
P.O. Michael GROGAN
P.O. Michael A. PER
P.O. Robert J. MENZ
P.O. Neil E. SAXTON
P.O. Victor CENTENO
SGT. James C. CLEVE
SGT. Glenn D. FRANK

May 9, 1992

David J. Bartholomew
Captain of Police
District Two
245 W. Lincoln Ave.
Milwaukee, Wi. 53215

Dear Captain Bartholomew;

   Our Block Association would like to commend your officers for the speedy response to a violent family disput that occurred on our street on May 6, at approximately 4:30 p.m. Many block members were outside at the time and observed the fight, several than calling 911. We watched as many patrol cars responsed and the officers quickly brought the situation under control, arresting four people.

   The current Directed Patrol Mission has been very visible in our neighborhood over the last week and our members overwhelming support these efforts. It is having a noticable effect on the activity level on our block and seems to be putting our "troublemak on notice. Our residents feel more secure and have expressed the hope that this Mission will continue through the summer to help insure a reduction in gang avitvities and violence as well as less property damage, graffiti, and vandalism. We want you to know your officers have our full support and co-operation. Our Association firmly believes in working along with the Police to make our neighborhood safe and we thank you for these extra effort with the directed Patrol Mission.

                                        Sincerely,

                                        The ████████████ Block Asso

                                        Block Co-Captain

2ND DISTRICT
RECEIVED
MAY 1 1992
CAPTAIN

93

GLENN D. FRANKOVIS

████████████████ BLOCK ASSOCIATION ·

ATTENTION: BLOCK WATCH PICNIC

The ████████████████. Block Watch will hold an end of
summer picnic on Sept. 27, from 1-6 P.M. at ████████████████.
All residents are cordially invited to attend. Please join us
for a picnic supper and socializing with your neighbors. Hopefull
we will have representatives from the Police Dept., the county
supervisor from our area, Tony Zelinski, and a representative
from the Mitchell Street Business Association. Non-alcoholic
refreshments and a main dish will be provided. We would appreciat
a passing dish from those attending. Residents can call ████
████████████ or ██████████ at ████████ to RSVP. We hope
to see all of our regular members and will welcome meeting those
that our new to our block.

The Block Watch Program has now been in existence on our
block for three years. We've been quite successful in our efforts
to reduce disorderly and nuisance behavior on our block. However,
there is still much that needs to be done in our neighborhood.
The Police are continuing their stepped up patrols in this area
that was begun in May, 1992. Their presence has been very welcome
during the summer and Captain Bartholomew from Second District
has assured us the Directed Patrol Mission(as it is called) will
continue in our area.

Attached is a Neighborhood Behavior Guideline sent out to
all Block Captains by Mayor Norquist. He has asked us to share
this with our members and feels that it can help us be good neighb
to each other and make our neighborhoods a place where we all
can enjoy living, We've been asked to review the guidelines
and consider using them within our onw block. Much of the guideli
are a common sense and courteous approach to living with close
neighbors. We will discuss the guidelines at the picnic. We
welcome all of your thoughts and ideas and can at that time decide
if we want to adopt this for our use.

Hope to see all of you on the 27!

████████████
Block Captains

Sept. 11. 1992

94

May 13, 1992

Capt. Bartholomew;

We reside in your district at ▬▬▬
▬▬▬▬▬▬▬

This letter is to let you know that as residents of this block, we have had the opportunity to see the new tactical force in action in regards to controlling street gang activities.

We, and our neighbors, are very impressed with the fast response to our calls, (especially in the last month) also with the fact that infractions with the law are being booked while at the same time we are not losing the officers on patrol.

We want to commend the officers involved and say to them; 'Thank you keep up the good work'.

Respectfully;
▬▬▬▬▬▬▬▬▬

Insp. Harken

GLENN D. FRANKOVIS

NEIGHBORHOOD BEHAVIOR GUIDELINES

. This is our neighborhood. We must work together to keep it a positive and safe place to be. The quality of life in our neighborhood depends on mutual respect and concern. We all must uphold a community standard.

. Noise can be an intrusion. Music from any source, including car stereos, is too loud if it can be heard two houses away, if it can be heard inside another house with windows closed, or if it interrupts another's activities. Please use common sense and be especially aware after 8:00 PM.

. Car horns are only to be used in emergency situations. They are not for announcing your arrival or attracting attention. This is the law. Please refrain from using yours in non-emergencies, and ask your guests and visitors to do the same.

. It's up to all of us to set a positive example in our neighborhood. Please be sure that language is not vulgar, violent or abusive. Remember that there are many small children in the area and speak appropriately.

. Alleys contain garbage, rocks, glass, and moving vehicles. They are not places for small children to play.

. Remember, the speed limit on residential streets is 25 MPH (and 15 MPH in alleys). Please drive carefully, and be mindful of the many children in our neighborhood.

. How we feel about our neighborhood has a lot to do with how our neighborhood looks. Overgrown weeds, eroded yards, trash anywhere (including in alleys), and generally uncared for property promote a negative image for our block. Let's all do our part to make this a block we can be proud of.

. Many of us have pets. If your pet spends time outside, please be sure to clean up after it, whether your yard or someone else's. Dogs should always be leashed, fenced, or supervised. The Humane Society should and will be called in the event of a loose animal.

9. Drugs will not be tolerated in our neighborhood. We must call the police anytime we detect the presence of drugs in this neighborhood. The stability of our neighborhood depends on this.

10. Landlords who do not live in the area need to be responsible
    neighbors as well. Please rent to people you would like to
    live next door to, and keep your property in the same condition
    you would if it were your home.

11. There is a gang problem in our neighborhood, though no on our
    block at this time. Since this is the case we need to be alert
    and act accordingly if we see suspicious activity or gang
    graffiti. Graffiti should be reported to the Police and than
    removed immediately.

12. We are fortunate to have an active Block Watch on our block.
    The only way to keep our neighborhood safe and secure is to
    keep our eyes open, report suspicious behavior, and know who
    our neighbors are. We cannot be afraid to get involved - it is
    the only way to create and maintain a good neighborhood.

Many of the problems mentioned can be solved with legal action.
Although we prefer to deal with problems at the neighborhood
level, we must be willing to report continuing situations to
the proper authorities.

GLENN D. FRANKOVIS

Close   Previous   Next   Forward   Reply to Sender   Reply All   Move   Delete   Read Later   Properties

From: ▓▓▓▓▓▓▓▓
To: Glenn Frankovis
Date: Wednesday - March 19, 2003 2:51 PM
Subject: Metcalf Park Happenings
📎   Mime.822 (3355 bytes) [View] [Save As]

Hello Captain,

I observed something very beautiful today. Around 11:30 a.m. I was leaving the office for lunch. While sitting in my car on North Avenue, I noticed a young male conversing with a female. In the process his pit bull was wandering aimlessly around. Then I noticed a squad car roll by. Much to my surprise the squad did a U-turn at the corner of 37th and North and addressed the male in words that I could not hear. The male grabbed his unleashed pit bull, who had just got through defecating on the vacant lot, by his collar and while stooping over, began to walk the dog. I sat there at least 3 to 4 minutes as the officers observed this guy struggling to move on with his dog.

Well, it was time for me to move on. As I turned the corner south on to 37th Street, I immediately observed a squad going south on the 2400 block of 37th street. I watched it until it turned east on Clarke Street, one of the areas busiest hangouts.

Man that was cool, with that level of police service, perhaps the Metcalfe Park Miracle is alive and well.

Keep up the good work!

LM
Metcalfe Park Residents' Association

THIRD DISTRICT
Received MAR 19 2003
Referred Roll Call Board
By Glenn D. Frankovis
Captain of Police

This message to me from Larry Moore is a true expression of appreciation for the service we are providing to the good people who live and work in District #3. The officers observed by Larry Moore were doing something that others may not have done. It was minor in the grand scheme of things, but it meant a lot to Larry Moore to see that we care.
Capt GDF 3/20

AREA SATURATION PATROL

St. Michael Parish
ACTS Program
1445 N. 24th Street
Milwaukee, Wisconsin 53205

St. Rose of Lima Parish
528 N. 31st Street
Milwaukee, Wisconsin 53208

Police Chief Arthur Jones
Police Administration Building
749 W. State Street
Milwaukee, Wisconsin 53208

May 15, 2003

Dear Chief Jones,

We are writing to you on behalf of the groups which meet regularly for *The Weed and Seed Project*. People from the parishes of St. Michael, St. Rose and the ACTS program meet with Captain Glenn Frankovis, other police officers and community service persons.

In the time that Captain Frankovis has been at District Three, we have seen a great improvement in the cooperation and interest of the police department to address the problems brought to their attention. Captain Frankovis is a man of action and a man of his word. Through his leadership, officers respond to a situation promptly and subsequent change for the positive is noticeable. Rarely is a second phone call necessary. Captain Frankovis shows that he cares about the people of the area.

Other service people from the city departments also follow through on requests for action promptly and thoroughly.

We are grateful for the community service all these persons provide; we look forward to working with them in the future. Thank you for your support.

Sincerely,
St. Michael Parish Community
ACTS Program
St. Rose Parish Community

cc: Captain Glenn D. Frankovis

THIRD DISTRICT
Received MAY 21 2003
Referred
By Glenn D. Frankovis

99

Community Partners

2100 W. Wells Street
Milwaukee, WI 53233
(414) 935-7868
Fax (414) 933-5030
www.cr-sdc.org

Oct. 7, 2002

Dear Captain Frankovis:

A+tached is a copy of INSITES, the Weed & Seed National magazine.

A Milwaukee article is on page 8 — with a smiling familiar face on page 9.

"One Milwaukee Night" is also featured on 10 & 11.

I know it's been a rough week. You are doing great work — don't stop. Let us know what else we can do —

Thanks —
Sue K.

Sue Kenealy, Program Manager
Matt Balistrieri, Program Supervisor

Mail Message

Close

Previous   Next   Forward   Reply to Sender   Reply All   Move   Delete   Properties

From: "Dennis Barrish"
To: Glenn Frankovis
Date: Saturday - March 16, 2002 2:11 PM
Subject: Community Drug Prevention Project - Neighborhood Victim Impact Statement

Mime.822 (4682 bytes) [View] [Save As]

Captain Frankovis:

A Marc Anthony type comment:

I was surprised to see that your district had 14 listings on the Victim Impact Statement for drug arrests based on up coming sentencing, while the district with the next highest amount of listings had only 4 listings for drug arrests. The dates of the 14 arrests were in December, immediately after your arrival.

What am I to think of that! I could look at it from several points of view. I choose to see that you are effectively managing a difficult problem in our area of the city.
Congratulations to you and your offices for your efforts in protecting us and making our neighborhoods saver. Some people do notice; both on paper and from personal experience. I have had numerous comments from persons living in our West End neighborhoods on the dramatic down turn in nuisance activity along 27th Street. Please keep up the great work you and your officers are doing for us. We thank you and we want you to know that we really do recognize and appreciate your efforts.

Dennis Barrish
West End Landlord Compact
West End Development Corporation

UNIFORM PATROL BUREAU
2002
Personnel Division
Dale J Schunk

Retain in Capt Frankvis file
c.c. N/C Edw Stenzel

GLENN D. FRANKOVIS

April, 19, 2002

Mr. Robert Samuels
Acting Director
US Department of Justice
Executive Office of Weed & Seed
810 Seventh Street, NW
Washington, DC 20531

Dear Mr. Samuels:

Thank you for the opportunity to submit a Milwaukee Weed & Seed nomination for the Coordination Honor Award Initiative. The Weed & Seed-Milwaukee project has generated a number of collaborative efforts in the past six years, many of which have resulted in the eradication of violent gang activity in the community. This has included the arrest and conviction of the Latin Kings and Lopez gangs, and the recent intervention and arrest of the "Murder Mob".

The nomination Milwaukee -Weed & Seed would like to present for consideration concerns a strong example of community/law enforcement collaboration known as OPERATION STREETSWEEPER. In this instance, two "prongs" of the Weed & Seed strategy joined together to work with and for residents to reduce street dealing and crime in the community.

In 2001, the 5th Milwaukee Police District (which has, in its geographical area, the Weed & Seed-United South sector), was assigned a new Captain, Glen Frankovis. Captain Frankovis, from the start of his tenure at the district, made a strong commitment to reduce "hot spots", areas in which there which crime and all its negative impact are especially virulent. At the same time, the Captain began to become familiar with the Community Partners Program. The Community Partners are employed and directed to distribute and explain resource information to residents in high crime areas. As the Partner gains trust and credibility in the community, residents often provide the Partner information which is valuable to the Milwaukee Police Department as well as other law enforcement entities (i.e., the Milwaukee HIDTA). The Partners have been acknowledged by law enforcement (local, state and federal) to be a reliable source of information regarding illegal activities in the community. In the same time frame, Captain Frankovis attended the Weed & Seed National Conference in Philadelphia (August of 2001), where he garnered additional information about the Weed & Seed strategy and philosophy.

The Captain, using crime data analysis, the reports from beat and car patrols, and information

102

from the Community Partners Program began to pinpoint and develop an interdictive strategy to eradicate known "hot spots". The Captain:

- developed an assignment schedule for personnel allocations which focused on "peak" crime times in those "hot spots",
- closely tracked the activities and conduct of those individuals who frequented those areas thus identifying problem behaviors, and
- consistently and routinely evaluated the hot spot activity and the incidence of crime in and around the area.

Using all the information sources, the Captain provided personnel and resources to intercede in those areas that were the most problematic. He implemented a number of neighborhood "sweeps", with sudden strike force patrols which surrounded hot spot participants at peak times of operation and quickly contained and arrested suspects.

The interdiction resulted in not only in quantifiable crime reduction, but an increase in the quality of life of those neighborhood residents who had suffered with the residual behaviors associated with drugs, guns and gangs. A number of illegal firearms were confiscated (several CEASEFIRE prosecutions were initiated under the "felon with a gun" law), offenders were arrested and convicted, drug houses shut down, street dealing was eliminated, but most important of all, the atmosphere of the neighborhood dramatically improved.

The Captain did not stop at just the statistics. He called on the Community Partners to assist in the process once again. The Community Partners, at the request of the Captain, developed and implemented a house to house survey which was facilitated in the "hot spot" areas within seven days of the interdiction. The following questions were asked of the residents:

- What is your perception/reaction to the recent actions of the Milwaukee Police Department?
- What else should be done by the MPD to make this a safe neighborhood?
- What other resources do you need? Housing repairs/loans? Safe Haven access? Adult education? Job skill or employment opportunities? Anything else?
- How can the MPD assist residents in the creation of or training of "block clubs?

The response of residents was overwhelmingly positive to the actions of the 5th District MPD. There were a variety of comments concerning peaceful nights because the gun shots had stopped, as well as relief that their children could play outside in the evening. Many residents expressed their appreciation to the department for its work, and provided additional information to the Community Partners which offered a foundation for continued investigations in the area. Residents were pleasantly surprised to hear that the MPD cared about their feelings and perceptions.

The comments from the residents were also shared with the MPD staff, who, for a change, were able to hear about the positive feedback from many residents about how pleased people were with the police department.

Captain Frankovis' innovative and creative strategy resulted in measurable and positive impacts on both a statistical and environmental levels in the 5th District. The response from the residents proved that these neighborhoods were truly more safe and secure because of STREETSWEEPER.

Captain Frankovis has since been re-assigned to the 3rd Milwaukee Police District. This district contains the Weed & Seed-North Project, and he has initiated STREETSWEEPER in this area as well. His successor at District 5 has continued the Streetsweeper strategy designed by Captain Frankovis which continues to include assistance from the Community Partners Program.

For these reasons, I strongly recommend that Captain Frankovis be recognized by Weed & Seed for the development of crime prevention and intervention concepts. He implemented a strategy in a practical and productive manner. An acknowledgment of his actions will not only send an appreciative message to the Captain, but will also encourage others in the law enforcement field to address crime in a proactive manner.

| Paul Henningsen
Alderman, 4th District | City Hall, Room 205
200 East Wells Street
Milwaukee, WI 53202-3570 | OFFICES
414-286-2221
414-286-3774
EMERGENCY
414-286-2150 | FAX
414-286-3456
EMAIL
pheni@ci.mil.wi.us | |

(kə lab′ə rāt′) collaborate

November 15, 2001

Captain Glen Frankovis
Third Police District
4715 West Vliet Street
Milwaukee, WI 53208

Dear Captain Frankovis:

Welcome to the Third. I look forward to working with you. Your great reputation regarding new ideas and community participation and involvement precedes you. I'll call in due course for an appointment.

Two items I'd like to bring to your attention now. 27th and Kilbourn (northwest corner) in front of and beside the store is the worst and seemingly most unsolvable pit of my district. Constant loitering and street dealing. Different actors at different times. Many don't carry but can "arrange" purchases elsewhere in the neighborhood. Many do not live in the neighborhood. Several hookers. Customers will drive up and walk up.

When we had beat or bicycle officers this crowd disappears and the whole of Kilbourn and 27th is calm and safe. This effective preventive policing, which I've personally pleaded with Chief Jones for (as well as Lucas countless times), doesn't seem to be a priority for reasons left unexplained to me, or should I say only unreasonably explained to me.

I sincerely hope you can fit them in, especially from 3:00 p.m. to 3:00 a.m.

Be that as it may, I have several suggestions for deterrence:

1.   Visibly take pictures of every bunch over a three-day period. Show to probation and parole officers. Many have paper forbidding them in area.

Paul Henningsen
Alderman, 4th District

City Hall, Room 205
200 East Wells Street
Milwaukee, WI 53202-3570

OFFICES
414-286-2221
414-286-3774
EMERGENCY
414-286-2150

FAX
414-286-3456
EMAIL
pheni@ci.mil.wi.us

(kə lab′ə rāt′) collaborate

Capt,

This has been the worst block in our entire district.

The people at 431 N. 29th seem to be the perpetrator.

Paul has asked this landlord to evict these people. Went to Court, the Judge said. they could stay.

The calls on This block, and the 400 block of 29th are driving me crazy.

What can we do about this situation?

Thanks Lucy

106

WASHINGTON HEIGHTS

Highlighter

WINTER 2004

To Catch a Thief

by Charlene Opie, Area Three Representative

Washington Heights is a community rich in character and charm, set among churches and schools that have anchored our neighborhood for nearly a century. This is a community that conjures up the truest sense of neighborhood. So this must be a community where residents are free from harm. But are we? The incidence of crime here among our beautiful bungalowed and bowered streets is low. There are ways for us to reduce it.

When there is a burglary here, we might wonder if the home or this neighborhood was targeted because of our location. Or we might conjecture that the Heights is an attractive target because of the beautiful and well-maintained housing stock, which may signify abundance. Rather than analyzing motivation, we should concentrate on protecting our homes and neighborhood by taking the advice of a former Milwaukee Police Department (MPD) Community

Liaison Officer, "We cannot control the desire or the ability of the criminal, but we can control the opportunity."

How? By being observant and proactive as was a resident earlier this year: As Barb went out to move her car from the curb to her driveway, she noticed a slow moving van, driven by two young men, on her street. She circled the block in her car and when she neared her home, discovered her neighbor in an altercation with one of the men from the van. Next, one of the men threw down her neighbor's child's bicycle and fled. When her neighbor began chasing the running man, she called 911. The other man left the scene before the officers arrived. Although the burglars escaped, Barb's call brought the police to the scene who took the report, alerted other officers about the men who fled the scene, and discovered that the van had been reported stolen.

[Beware! Captain Frankovis strongly advises that it is far safer and wiser for residents to call 911, when they discover a crime in progress, than to try to apprehend the perpetrators.]

In addition to making direct reports to the police, when you see suspicious activity, each of us in the Heights can bolster individual effort through the collective strength of the Block Watch groups. Did you know that the Washington Heights Neighborhood Association has an active Block Watch Committee, whose goal is to establish and amplify communication between the Third District Police Department, Block Watch

Captain Frankovis:
Real Time and Interactive

Third District Police Captain Frankovis wants to hear from you. He urges residents to call him, (yes, *call him*) whenever you hear or see something that seems unusual or suspicious in your alley, or when you know that a crime's been committed in the Heights. "The only way I can be effective is if I know what's going on out there," he told the *Highlighter*. "Call me." He picks up the phone when you call 935-7230, Monday through Friday. Reach him by fax at 935-7113. You can make your call anonymously. The captain is earnest about his desire to work directly with residents. This is a rare opportunity to get first hand help from the person in charge of this district.

Captains, and individual residents, house-by-house, and block-by-block? Individual involvement, like Barb's, can truly impact crime! If we all were to be as observant and proactive, we would further reduce the incidence of crime.

Here are some ways you might play an integral part:

1. Access WHNA's list serve, **www.groups.yahoo.com/group/ washington heights**, to read posted crime reports to find out what might be

continued on page 12

<table>
MARK YOUR CALENDAR

January 15
Mayoral Candidate Forum
Washington Park Senior Center
6:30–8:30 pm

February 2
Block Watch & Safety Meeting
6:30 pm–8:30 pm
Washington Park Senior Center

March 27
Easter Egg Hunt Registration
10 am–2 pm
Washington Park Senior Center

April 3
Easter Egg Hunt
Washington Park
</table>

KERSHEK LAW OFFICES

NOT A PARTNERSHIP

EUGENE A. KERSHEK

E. JOSEPH KERSHEK
COURT COMMISSIONER

JENNIFER L. ANDERSON

SUITE 201 ASSOCIATED BANK BUILDING
10701 WEST NATIONAL AVENUE
MILWAUKEE, WI 53227-3239
Email: kersheklaw@aol.com
PHONE: (414) 321-6530
FAX: (414) 321-6535

August 8, 2002

Milwaukee Police Department
District No. 3
4715 W. Vliet
Milwaukee, WI 53233
Attention: Capt. Frank Ovis
Dear Captain:

I want to thank you for the ASP Group and Sgt. Chris Brown for the great job they are doing on W. Wells Street, Milwaukee.

I own a 20 family building at 3306 W. Wells and a 16 family at 3401 W. Wells Street. I am trying to eliminate problems in that area and I sincerely appreciate your office helping me. You do a great job in crime prevention.

Sincerely,

Eugene A. Kershek

cc: Richard Lucas

UNIFORM PATROL BUREAU
9/4/02
PERSONNEL DIVISION
Dale J Schunk
Deputy Chief

THIRD DISTRICT
Received AUG 27 2002
Referred PATROL BUREAU
D/C SCHUNK
By Glenn D. Frankovis
Captain of Police

02 SEP 10 AM 8: 26
MILWAUKEE POLICE DEPT.
PERSONNEL DIVISION

I THOUGHT YOU MIGHT SHARE THIS WITH THE CHIEF & ASST CHIEF.

REFERENCES

[i] Milwaukee Journal Sentinel, 07-07-2011 "Response to Riverwest Attack not Police Department's 'Finest Hour', Flynn Says"

[ii] AP Article 12-20-2013 "Unprovoked Attacks at Heart of 'Knockout King', by Jim Salter (AP)

[iii] Milwaukee Journal Sentinel, 12-29-2011, Social Media Helps Prevent Mayfair Disturbance"

[iv] New York Daily News, 12-06-2013, - Denis Hamill – "Returning NYPD Commissioner Bill Bratton will keep Stop-and-Frisk – but Target the Real Criminals"

[v] Rolling Stone Magazine, 12-11-2013, "Apocalypse, New Jersey: A Dispatch from America's Most Desperate Town" by Matt Taibbi

[vi] Rolling Stone Magazine, 12-11-2013, Same article by Matt Taibbi

[vii] Knight-My Story, by Coach Bob Knight – page 71

[viii] Knight-My Story – Page 348

[ix] Milwaukee Journal Sentinel, 11-27-1994 citing a New York Times, AP report: Patrols getting guns off streets

[x] Milwaukee Police Department Standard Operating Procedures (SOP) on Summary Arrests, General Order #2022-03, pages 16-18, 3/075.00 – 3/075.15

[xi] Crime Fighter, by Jack Maple

[xii] War as I knew It, by General George S. Patton

[xiii] Nomination Letter Recommending Operation Street Sweeper for national award given out by the D.O.J – Executive Office of Weed and Seed

[xiv] District #5 Charts and Stats for 2001-2002

[xv] Weed & Seed In-Sites Magazine, Summer 2002, describing Operation Street Sweeper and recognizing the Milwaukee Police Department's District #5 implementation of same in 2001 (One of only 5 Police Departments in the country to receive the award titled: Law Enforcement Coordination Honor Award for calendar year 2001 and presented at the Weed & Seed Task Force Coordination Conference in New Orleans, Louisiana on June 19, 2002

[16] U.S. Supreme Court Case Terry v. Ohio, 392 U.S. 1 argued December 12, 1967 and Decided on June 10, 1968

[17] FBI Law Enforcement Bulletin, January 1995, Cruising for Trouble: Gang-Related Drive-By Shootings, by Roger H. Davis, Ph.D.

[18] www.theatlantic.com/magazine/archive/1982/03/broken-windows/304465/ also Law Enforcement News, Vol. XXIX, Nos. 611, 612 dated December 15/31, 2003 As Clear as Glass: With the "Broken Windows" thesis, and Civic Report 22: December 2001 Do Police Matter? An Analysis of the Impact of New York City's Police Reforms by Senior Fellow, The Manhatten Institute for Policy Research, William H. Sousa, jr., Director of Evaluation, Police Institute, Rutgers University

[19] Knight-My Story, by Coach Bob Knight, page 17

[20] Leaders-The Strategies For Taking Charge, by Warren Bennis & Burt Nanus

[21] <u>Knight-My Story,</u> page 280

[22] <u>Leadership,</u> by Mayor Rudolph W. Giuliani, page 41

ADDITIONAL REFERENCES

- In the Line of Fire: Violence Against Law Enforcement – A Study of Felonious Assaults on Law Enforcement Officers by Anthony j. Pinizzotto, Ph.D. FBI Training Division – Behavioral Sciences Unit; Edward F. Davis, MS   FBI Training Division – Behavioral Sciences Unit; and Charles E. Miller III   FBI Criminal Justice Information Services Division – Education/Training Service Unit   (FBI Publication #0163 October 1997) http://www.fbi.gov/stats-services/publications/law-enforcement-bulletin/january-2010/the-fbi2019s-national-law-enforcement-safety-initiative   and   Street   Gang Mentality   http://www.fbi.gov/stats-services/publications/law-enforcement-bulletin/2007-pdfs/sept07leb.pdf
- The   Broken   Windows   Theory   of   Policing   (http://www.manhattan-institute.org/pdf/_atlantic_monthly-broken_windows.pdf)   James Q. Wilson and George L. Kelling
- http://www.theatlantic.com/magazine/archive/1982/03/broken-windows/304465/
- The Crime Fighter: How You Can Make Your Community Crime-Free by Jack Maple with Chris Mitchell Broadway Books New York
- War As I Knew It: General George S. Patton jr Houghton-Miflin (page 357)
- My Story by Bob Knight with Bob Hammel, Thomas Dunne Books 2002
- SCOTUS   Decision   on   Summary   Arrest   for   Municipal   Ordinance   Violations http://biotech.law.lsu.edu/cases/pp/atwater.htm
- Famous Quotes from General George S. Patton jr
- http://www.generalpatton.com/quotes/index.html
- Leaders: The Strategies for Taking Charge, Warren Bennis & Burt Nanus, Harper & Row, publishers
- <u>Other books by Bennis:</u>
- Why Leaders Can't Lead: The Unconscious Conspiracy Continues   Jossey-Bass Publishers
- Organizing Genius: The Secrets of Creative Collaboration, by Warren Bennis & Patricia Ward Biederman, Perseus Books
- The Future of Leadership, by Warren Bennis, Gretchen M. Spreitzer, & Thomas G. Cummings,   Jossey-Bass publishers

NOTES

NOTES

NOTES

NOTES

NOTES

NOTES

NOTES